Executive conference room wall.

NICE COUNTRY, AMERICA!

THE PETER NAPOLI STORY, FROM SICILY TO NEW ENGLAND

PETER NAPOLI

NICE COUNTRY, AMERICA!
THE PETER NAPOLI STORY, FROM SICILY TO NEW ENGLAND

Image Citations:
Coat of Arms. *Civic Heraldry*. Pietraperzia. https://www.araldicacivica.it/wp-content/uploads/2016/04/Pietraperzia-A-218x300.jpg

All other images:
Napoli, Peter. Author's personal collection.

DISCLAIMER AND/OR LEGAL NOTICES

DEDICATION

To my parents, Salvatore and Lucia Napoli:

As my father always reminded us,
Fare del bene agli altri, per poi dimenticarsene.

You were right. Thanks, Dad.

And to my grandchildren,
Peter, Sophia, Jake, Chloe, Nolan, Colin, and Hazel:

In time, as they wonder about their grandparents,
I hope this book will give them some insight into their heritage.

– P. S. N.

TABLE OF CONTENTS

PART I: My Story

PART II: Rules for Success

FOR YOUR CAREER

FOR YOURSELF

AFTERWORD

INTRODUCTION

My name is Peter Salvatore Napoli. I was born May 16, 1950, in the town of Pietraperzia in central Sicily. My mother and father brought me to America in 1963. It has been my home ever since.

If you're reading this, you probably know me: you may be my child, grandchild, great-grandchild, or one of their offspring. You may also be family, a friend, an acquaintance, a business colleague – or even a customer!

Whoever you are, and whatever brought you to these pages, I'm pleased that you're here.

This is my story, the tale of a family coming to America, then of my building a life that has been, in a word, wonderful. It's also the story of a career, a business, and a home – in the biggest sense of that word.

Most of all, it is the story of seeing what's important in life by believing as much in others as you believe in yourself.

Let me tell you my tale.

PART 1: My Story

Nice Country, America!

MY FATHER'S DREAM (1957–1963)

I come from Sicily. My family roots run deep there.

From the moment I stepped off the plane as a teenage immigrant arriving in New England, I knew, from then on, I would be an American. But there will always be a lot of Sicily in me.

As I look back on my life, I remember many nights I spent dreaming of my first country, my first home. I still have those dreams. Sometimes my mind takes me to the things I've seen on visits there. More often, those dreams are filled with the people, places, and events I've heard in stories my family told me. I will always dream of Sicily, a faraway place in my past.

But over a half-century ago, my father dreamed, too. He dreamed of America… and the future.

* * *

Pietraperzia, the town in central Sicily that is the place of my birth in the middle of the 20th century, was farming country then and remains so. Families have grown the same crops for generations, mostly wheat and almonds.

The problem is that not everybody born and raised in Pietraperzia wants to stick around to farm. Over the years, young people have emigrated to northern Italy, Germany, America, and beyond.

Other than agriculture and the nice people, there isn't much to keep a young person in Pietraperzia.

My father was one of those who left, though it took him until age 48 to make the move. When he brought us to America in 1963, I was 13 years old. The population of the little town we were leaving was about 15,000. A few years ago, I spoke with a cousin who was trying to sell his parents' home there. I asked how the sale was going.

"How much do you have in your pocket?" he said. "Whatever that is, Peter, you can have it."

Few people live there anymore. Fewer want to. The population has dwindled to about 5,000 souls.

Naturally, wanting to find different things to do with your life does not mean the life you're leaving is bad. After all, my dad did not leave Sicily because it was not a wonderful place – it was: We lived a comfortable life, at least that's the way I saw it as a kid; this is how I remember it today and always have. Dad took us out of Sicily in pursuit of more opportunities than our village offered – more than Europe offered, too. There was nothing to compare to what you could do in America. That's true today, and it was true then. If you don't believe me, just visit some other parts of the world, as I have. When it comes to opportunity, America is as good as it gets.

Dad wanted to take advantage of that opportunity.

* * *

If you had to choose one word to describe my father, that word would be *ambitious*. Only a few people find a way to turn their ambition into success. My father succeeded early on because he had an advantage: his ambition was matched with creativity and a willingness to work hard.

As soon as he was old enough to get a job, he did. He started in the family business, making clay roof shingles alongside his two brothers. They made the shingles by starting with a mud pit, throwing hay in there, then forming the bricks and baking them in an oven. It was unpleasant, tedious, hot work – dirty stuff.

In time, he moved on to other businesses, eventually finding a way to make money from the local agriculture business without having to farm himself. He bought crops from farmers and stored them in warehouses so he could sell them to big commercial buyers who were interested in buying what they needed in a single transaction, which was more than just one farmer could supply. He did okay with that, but he was still finding his way, trying to figure out how to be even more creative – and profitable – in business. In time, he moved on to real estate. If somebody had a farm for sale, my dad would try to develop it into a useful parcel or property so he could sell it again at a profit. Later he obtained a license – a quite expensive license – to open a *tabaccheria*, a place that is sanctioned by the government for the sale of cigarettes and tobacco products. His tabaccheria was also a little variety store, with candy and such. My mom helped.

Some of my father's interest in America must have come from his older sister. She had immigrated to the US years before, probably to get away from the poverty so common for farming families where we lived. She and Dad kept in touch. Having her in America must have been tantalizing for him. He was in a small town while she was in a big, unknown place far away. That leaves a lot of room for imagination to fill in the blanks, and an ambitious man generally fills in what he doesn't know with optimism for what might be.

Back then, the United States was the only destination for those with a dream of "something more." My father was happy to put faith in his hope. I'll say it plain: he thought of America as the place where dollars grow on trees. You could have a good – or good enough – life in Europe in general and Sicily in particular, but he believed that if you could get to America, you could have much more. You could even become wealthy.

This was not because he thought America was a place where they just handed things to you. He thought of America as the land of plenty, sure, but he meant plenty of *opportunity*, where someone willing to work hard and look for ways to get ahead would find those ways. He wasn't alone in this belief. We all were confident that America was a place where the work ethic gets rewarded. It gives away nothing to tell you that this story ends with a wonderful validation of this belief, but back then it was only faith and hope.

* * *

There was another reason to come to America or, at least, to leave Sicily, and that was the corruption – but it's not what you think. When I use the words "Sicily" and "corruption" in the same sentence, you probably imagine sepia-toned mob movies and tough guys in fedoras and shiny suits. In the movies, there is a coordinated "racket" where one "family" controls this "pie" and another family controls another. But where we were, it wasn't like that, at least as I remember it. Some people had to pay "protection money," sure, and the local government certainly had dubious elements (more on that later), but my dad avoided all that. To my knowledge, Dad never paid anybody over his tabaccheria, to name just one of his businesses.

When I say that corruption was a reason for us to leave, I mean that doing business was rarely based solely on merit and honest competition. There was a lot of "it's not what you know, it's who you know," a lot of bureaucracy that existed solely to propagate itself. Many problems were entirely artificial. They existed only because there was money to be made erecting roadblocks to a given project. They were toll booths to collect payoffs just for getting out of the way.

It's funny how those mob movies are always caught up in "respect." My dad, with no mob connections whatsoever, was very well respected. Perhaps that was because he showed such respect to other people. This alone helped me see that the best way to get along in life is to be nice to people, to be fair, and to be honest in your dealings with everyone.

Our life in Pietraperzia was comfortable and happy. Dad owned property and had business interests. He was one of the first people in the town to own an automobile by the early 60s, which meant we could go places. My cousins used to make fun of us as if we were spoiled city kids, but we loved spending time out of the city, often on our grandfather's farm. Most people lived off the land. If you didn't have much, this was not a bad way to get along. If figs were in season, you ate a lot of figs. If oranges were in season, you ate a lot of oranges. My grandfather had lots of fruit trees: every morning we were with him in the country, he would have fresh fruit for breakfast for us.

Even if things had been perfect in Sicily, my dad would have set his sights on America anyway. He wasn't running from a problem. He was running toward an opportunity. Whether we would come to America was a settled issue. What was not settled was who would go and when.

* * *

The truth, though it was rarely spoken, was that not everyone in our family of six wanted us to go. Dad was worlds beyond the rest of us in terms of enthusiasm. By habit, or maybe to bolster his confidence, he had come to believe that America truly was the land of milk and honey. I'm not sure George Washington was as excited about America as Dad was.

So my concern was not that I could talk him out of going. That wasn't going to happen. And of course, as a kid, a part of me was quite excited.

A big part of me was afraid. Could we make the transition? Could I? I knew I could adjust, more or less. But would I ever fit in, really? I would have to find my way in a different culture and learn a new language, and that was just for starters. There would be other demands that I couldn't yet imagine. I was so nervous that even though I was just a kid I lost some of my hair.

So I was secretly pleased when my father announced that he would first go by himself. He'd scope out America, get the lay of the land. That would include finding work – not just something to carry us from paycheck to paycheck but something that he could count on. He had to be able to take care of his family. We would also need a place to live. He would do all that, then send for us, maybe even return triumphantly to accompany us back to America.

My mother was having none of it. "Either all of us go, or none of us," she said.

Looking back, I see now that my mother had the right idea. This was the smart move, going together, because there were challenges we could not have foreseen. To overcome them, Dad would need us there, sometimes for emotional support but more often for the extra hands and a few key, practical skills he did not have. Even working together, getting the papers and permissions to do this or that, took my parents several years. Had my father gone over first and done everything on our behalf, our family would have been separated for a significant portion of our growing-up years – not a good thing, not at all. I'm glad they did it the way they did, and I'm glad my mother insisted on "all or nothing."

There was another problem to be overcome, too. In those days if you wanted to come to America you had to have a sponsor – someone to guarantee that if you came over and, God forbid, you weren't able to find work and support yourself, this person would promise to provide for your needs. This sponsorship had to be formalized as a written document, a contract. My father's sister had come over years before when she was about 17, so when she left, my father was just a child of 5 or 6. Because of that, they didn't really know each other. She wouldn't be able to be our guarantor, and I can't say that I blame her. My father was a stand-up guy, but she didn't have any way to be sure of that, and making a promise to support someone else, let alone a family, was a huge commitment.

However, I also had a great-uncle, Salvatore Salamone, the brother of my mother's father, making him my mother's uncle. He had come to this country, too, along with his nephew, Santo Salamone. When Uncle Salvatore learned that we wanted to come over, he offered to sponsor us. He said he would take us in until we were able to find an apartment in this country.

* * *

So my father's move to America wasn't the first in our family. But the history went much further back than the previous ten or twenty years.

My mother's parents had come to America in the early 1900s. On that side of the family, my grandmother was named Concetta and my grandfather was named Pietro, like me, Pietro Salamone. (I changed my name to Peter, the American version of the name when I became an American citizen.) Though I never met my father's parents, I spent quite a bit of time with my grandfather Pietro and his relatives.

If you're reading closely, you may be asking this: *if Grandfather Pietro had already come to America, how were you spending time with him in Sicily?* Grandfather Pietro came to America for the same reason we eventually would a half-century later: to find work and to make a better life. When he was here, he lived in Springfield, Massachusetts, and worked for the railroad, but after a while, his father became sick and needed his son to come back to the old country and help run the farm, which he did.

It must have been a tough decision – not in terms of whether to help his father but in terms of what he was leaving behind, and what he would be returning to do. Running a farm – in those days – was real labor, hard work. You would turn the ground with a mule and plow, or you did it by hand. It was tough and that is why a lot of people didn't want to do it. These days, it is all done by machinery, but not then. My grandfather would leave home at four or five in the morning and come back at six or seven at night. When he got home, there would be a big dish of pasta – he was too exhausted most nights for much of anything else.

Pietro loved America, and I remember the many times we would talk about coming over to America. He would tell me, "You go over, you work hard, and then they'll make you boss." That was his impression of America, and since he had been there already, I believed him. It was a powerful vision and a powerful motivator then – and it still is today. He understood that a lot of people, probably most people in America, really do recognize hard work, positive attitude, and initiative. So even though he would be losing us, saying goodbye to part of his family – his grandchildren – he encouraged us to go to America to make a better life. Perhaps he thought we might pick up where he left off.

Thus my father's idea to bring us to America was a move toward something promising and new – this brave move was already in our blood. Seeking to do better was a family tradition.

This time, the move to America would stick.

COMING TO AMERICA (1963–1966)

We arrived in this country in June 1963 through Boston's Logan Airport.

Our first stop was the home of my father's sister. She had a magnificent place in Arlington Heights, Massachusetts, a wonderful community then as it is now. Boy, were we impressed! She had indoor plumbing, which was unusual back in Sicily. She even had more than one bathroom!

I remember thinking, *Wow, this is living.*

It would have been a lovely place for us to stay while we settled into America, but my aunt was not comfortable hosting us, and I don't fault her. She had a big house, but it wasn't so big that a family of six could just move in with room left for her own family and her day-to-day life.

So, as planned, we went to see Salvatore, who had promised to sponsor us. He was a man so critical in helping us get started that it is fair to say I wouldn't be here today without him. He took us in while we looked for somewhere to live, as he said he would.

Finding a place of our own was an adventure. When we went to look at apartments, we all went together. That posed a problem. We'd show up at the door, and the potential landlord would take one look at our huge family and tell my folks that they didn't want six people living in their place. It was too many people in general and too many kids in particular; that was the typical response. Of course, we were willing to be crowded up even if we didn't want to be, but most of these landlords weren't having it. Unlike today, with the rules and laws in place about non-discrimination, we were at the mercy of the people we met. It was both humbling and insulting to go from having a nice place to live to having people look right in your face and reject you. I can say it built character, but it was very discouraging. Once again, I lost some hair because of the stress!

Now Santo would come to the rescue. He had a "triple-decker" property, and the third floor happened to be open. He said we could rent it from him. At last! Someone who welcomed a big family with lots of kids. Even better, he and his wife had children too, and we would be able to play with them. Their kids could even speak a little Italian, enough at least for kids to carry on and have fun.

Their rental was a modest place, maybe a thousand square feet, with a single bathroom we'd have to share, but he would let us rent it, and we were glad to have it.

(As an aside: a few years ago I was invited to speak to a meeting of the Sons of Italy. I wanted to mention that my bedroom is now bigger than the place we first lived in. My wife said I should rethink that comment: "Some people live in a thousand square feet with six people, so maybe you ought not say anything. You don't want to boast." She was right, as usual.)

So we settled into our third-floor apartment, crowded together but happy to have a place to call our own and pleased to be together.

* * *

In short order, we all went to work, everybody chipping in to provide the things a family needs, plus saving money for a home of our own.

My dad brought in the main measure of financial security, working a back-breaking 12 hours a day, sometimes more, six days a week. This, you should know, was typical for Italian immigrants like him. Sunday was a "lighter" day, although it wasn't that much lighter: 8 hours, what other people would consider a full day. But he cut it short – short for him – so we could have a nice dinner as a family and spend time together.

My mother worked hard too. She prepared all the meals, took care of our home, and raised children, but there was more. She also took on a full-time job. It was hardly a traditional role for a mother at the time, but it was right for us. She worked as a seamstress in the Asher Pants factory on Airport Road in Fitchburg, a job she held until she retired decades later.

The kids who were old enough went to work as well. My sister, Rosa, joined my mother at the pants factory. My oldest brother, Phil, who had gone to college a bit in Sicily, deferred returning to school so he could help us pay our bills. (He would return to school later and become an engineer.) My younger brother, Joe, was only eight so he didn't get a job. His job was being a kid.

Because I was 13 years old, I went to school and worked when the opportunity arose. My Uncle Salvatore had a son, Phil, who did landscaping and mowing and offered to take me on. We had not been in America long when I went to work for him, cutting grass at people's homes. I was glad for the opportunity. However, it led to an incident I've never forgotten.

We were cutting the grass at a home I thought was a magnificent place. Of course, in those days I had not seen much of the world or much of anything, so everything seemed magnificent to me. I was there working, a small kid, very thin, and I probably weighed no more than 120 pounds. The property owner of this "magnificent" place came out and said to Phil, "Look, I'm not going to pay you for this kid working. It doesn't look like he can do much in the first place."

We were on a break when this happened, and the man said it with me standing there. I thought, "So much for that! I'm not going to get paid for working." The guy wanted my cousin, and he had no intention of paying both of us, especially not me.

Yet at the end of the day, my cousin Phil paid me. Whether the man paid Phil for what I did, I can't say, but I'm pretty sure the guy stiffed him. Phil took care of me anyway, and because of the circumstances and the times the guy could get away with it.

I've never forgotten that day, being at the mercy of the "haves" while you're one of the "have nots," or at least one of the "has less than they'd like." The lesson I gleaned from this experience was this: appreciate people, no matter who they are. It's the right thing to do, and you have to do the right thing. You pay people right. You treat them right. You show kindness and generosity.

These days I hire a lot of people – by the thousands. That lesson is at the top of what I do: treat people right. Back home at my own "magnificent" place, I'm also the guy who hires the landscapers. I wish that somehow the guy who hired Phil and me could see how things turned out – not to rub his nose in it, but so he might know that there's a better way. Yet his bad behavior spawned a lot more good behavior. The tables have turned.

Do right by folks. Be courteous and friendly. When someone is sweating in the summer sun, offer them a drink of water. Invite them into the shade. And share a kind word. It's just the right thing to do. It's what makes the world go around.

* * *

My first day of work was tough, but my first day of school was tougher.

Arriving in the US and not being able to speak English was hard for everyone in my family, but it was especially tough for me at age 13. These days there are many resources to smooth the transition, especially to help children who don't speak English. Back then, it was sink or swim – mostly sink. In public school, they put you in a class and everybody hoped for the best.

I remember that first day. My parents could not miss work, so I had to go to school by myself. To make things more difficult, since all I've ever known is the culture of the country I came from, I was dressed differently from the other children. At that age, it's already hard to fit in. The little things we take for granted can easily be a big deal to an immigrant: the simple social cues that locals catch aren't obvious to those who are fresh off the boat. I remember there was an older woman my mother knew, a woman who happened to be from our hometown in Sicily, and she told my mother that kids ought to have sneakers. They went shopping and found some sneakers on sale to get for me, but the lady didn't realize that these sneakers were for girls. When I saw them, I thought maybe something was a little off, but I chalked it up as one more thing I had yet to learn about America.

Wrong! I went to school in those sneakers thinking that's what was in style, and you can't imagine the abuse I took. Of course, my mother was just trying to do her best for me. The fact that she cared enough to buy me sneakers and was willing to sacrifice in this way showed how much she loved me because the family priority was to be as conservative as possible with our money just so we could get along.

It was hard to make friends. We were different. I was ready to move back to Sicily. I was so nervous in all of this, so stressed all the time, that I continued to lose my hair. (Fortunately, it came back.)

Yet there were hopeful things that happened, too. I had a very good teacher, Mrs. Harrington, at my first school, the Nolan School of Fitchburg. She helped me to learn the language, even giving me her own time during lunches. She was a wonderful person.

When we moved to the new house and I had to change schools again, I began the day at the principal's office to register. Once again, I attended the first day all by myself because my parents could not miss work. But this time, I had rehearsed a little arrival speech – just a line so I could tell the principal that I was new. The problem was that I was so nervous that I forgot my line. Instead of telling him I was a new student, I told him I was just "new."

"No you're not!" he laughed. "You're at least 14 years old!" His name was Mr. Antonioni, and he turned out to be a very nice fellow.

* * *

We continued to make a place for ourselves in America in ways big and small. Coming from Sicily, food was a big deal to us, and going to the grocery store was a part of that.

The market was a little over a mile from our third-floor apartment home. My mother, my younger brother, and I would make the trip on foot. We didn't have a car, and, even if we had had one, none of us had a driver's license. It wasn't a good use of our limited funds to take a taxi either, so after we walked to the store and bought our things, we would walk back again, carrying our bags in our arms. My younger brother, who was not yet ten years old, didn't think anything of this. But as a boy in my very early teens, this was all very embarrassing for me. As an adult looking back, I realize of course that it wasn't a big deal. But when you're a kid, it is. It certainly was for me.

Whether what I remember now really happened, I can't say, but I remember people staring at us when we left the store on foot while they got in their cars and drove away. Then I remember walking down the sidewalk and seeing people stare at us along the way, a mother and her two boys carrying enough groceries for a family of six, and a family that ate well at that. Whether people noticed us or it was only in my mind, it was still quite a hike.

As for the food we brought home on these trips, my mother turned it into something amazing every time. She was a great cook, and could make a really great meal from nothing. She bought ingredients. Nothing we ate was made outside her kitchen. She made homemade pasta – obviously, she did because we're Italian. She made tremendous sauces, too. Mom learned to cook as a girl and then as a young woman, staying home with her mother to help prepare meals, including baking. It was all exceptional in flavor and taste. Her use of spices was wonderful, and her abilities with meats and vegetables are something I remember to this day. It's difficult – no, make that impossible – for me to describe my favorite meals of hers because she made so many different things and they were all so very good. She made a variety of pasta. She made dishes with chicken, lamb, and veal – not much beef, but with so much else to enjoy it never crossed my mind. Of course, being from Sicily meant we had a long tradition of delicious fish meals, and she made those too.

Years later, I would sometimes stop by for lunch since I worked in the area. I would appear at the door with no notice, and it seemed she would disappear into her kitchen for only a minute or two, then emerge with a magnificent lunch apparently out of nowhere. Of course, this would be far beyond the normal quick lunch of, say, a sandwich and a bowl of soup. For instance, she might produce a beautiful tomato salad with red onions, cheese, olives, and more – and always, always, with fresh bread. To this day, that's probably my favorite meal, though these days I'll pair it with a nice glass of red wine.

* * *

Another thing that helped us become more comfortable in America was to start joining in some of the traditions. Some were small and carried over naturally from Sicily. For instance, we walked to church as a family every Sunday, though I always thought it was funny that my father could be praying one minute and then swearing about something the next.

We discovered the larger, more uniquely American traditions as well, but the problem for an immigrant family is that you don't know what you don't know – meaning that when the holiday arrives, it's not that you don't want to celebrate it. It's that you didn't know you could.

Take, for instance, Thanksgiving. In Sicily, there's no such thing. I remember our first Thanksgiving in 1963. We were starting from scratch. Our relatives who owned the building were our source of information, and they told my mother that turkey was the traditional dish. They also told her how she might prepare it. But it didn't matter, because we all decided immediately that we didn't like the taste of turkey and would much rather have chicken if the holiday required eating poultry. I guess we had been spoiled by my mother's ability to cook everything else.

Regardless, we had great traditions at home with our immediate and extended family. We always had wonderful celebrations, and if Thanksgiving wasn't an immediate hit for us, there were many other holidays that we loved that bring fond memories to this day. Christmas was lovely, of course, but it wasn't as big for us in those days as it was for most families with a long tradition in America. I think that's because where we came from, in Sicily, most families didn't have a great deal of money to spend on gifts. For us, it was just a holiday, but "just a holiday" can be misleading. For us, a holiday was a wonderful and welcome opportunity to get together, enjoy each other's company, and eat delicious food.

My dad started other traditions for us to do as a family, such as making homemade wine. If you've ever done it or even attempted, you know that it's a lot of hard work. A few years ago, I tried to pick up the tradition again when my son got married. I tried to make some homemade wine as a gift to our guests. Holy smokes! It was even harder than I remembered. Maybe next time I'll just call Amazon.

No matter the holiday, we celebrated each other's company. Birthdays were big and still are. To give us something to look forward to, and to tamp down some of the homesickness we all felt, we began to save money for a trip back to Sicily that we took only a few years later. There are certain connections of habit and heart that, if you don't keep them up, you simply lose them.

* * *

Dad was certain he could do well in America. He expected to achieve it by doing here what he had done at home: going into business. It didn't work out that way. He arrived speaking no English, so he put his entrepreneur's dreams on hold for a bit while he tried to get his feet under himself, so to speak. With a family to support, he went to work right away, first in a plastics shop and later in a company that made boxes. There were other jobs as well, and lots of overtime into the night – all to keep us fed, clothed, and covered with a roof over our heads.

His early attempts at business didn't work out. One of his first ventures was a construction business. He was robbed of his life savings – for a while.

My father partnered with a couple of men who were building homes. Dad put in significant money to finance the development, which seemed like a promising investment. But he suffered the fate that so many other newly arrived immigrants suffered: he was taken advantage of by people who preyed on his lack of experience in a new country. They had at best misrepresented their project and at worst had never intended to build anything at all. They didn't produce results. They produced excuses. Dad quickly realized that his money was gone, nearly his entire life savings.

It's hard to imagine how terrified he must have felt. He had come here leaving everything behind. He didn't know the culture or the business world, and these two men had robbed him of everything.

But Dad was not one to take such a thing lying down. He didn't know exactly how the American system works, but he figured it out.

Not long after, he visited the office of the attorney general, bringing my older brother and me along to translate and perhaps for a little moral support. I was still in high school, yet here I was in this office mediating between my father and this important public official. My father showed him all the documents and financial records the men had shared with him, and it was obvious to the official that this was a dishonest deal.

To this day, I don't quite know how Dad did it. I was the translator, and I still don't know! The attorney general was able to get back nearly all of my father's money. His life savings and the financial safety net for our family were restored.

* * *

Dad's challenges with culture and language convinced me to plan ahead and do things to smooth my way. When I became a citizen, I Americanized my name. I figured it was pretty simple: I'm in America, I need to be an American. I wasn't rejecting my heritage then, and I don't reject it now. I'm proud to be Italian, but you have to bloom where you're planted.

There couldn't be a more miserable thing than to go to some place and make a conscious decision to reject their ways in favor of the ways of the place you came from. Why in the world would you make the switch in the first place if you didn't intend to be a part of this new world, this new adventure?

All this may sound like a trial, especially for a young man. I guess it was, yet I'm grateful every day for it. What an experience, to start over in a new place and to know, even at a young age, that what I was doing – what all we kids were doing – mattered in terms of making a way for our family.

Those days were a great experiment. Wherever we would go, I got to meet people from many and various backgrounds, often quite different from my own. It made me aware of just how big the world is – and how filled it is with possibilities.

I was especially intrigued by the people that I thought were "super" rich. Of course, they weren't super rich at all – if they had been, they wouldn't have lived in my neighborhood. But I noticed their big homes, at least big to me as a boy living in a much smaller home, and I noticed that they could afford to have someone else cut their lawn. We had to cut our own lawn, though looking back now I should have appreciated that we had a lawn at all. I would often daydream about someday having one of these homes. I wanted mine to have a horseshoe driveway. If you're going to dream, might as well dream big.

* * *

We pooled our money to save for a place we could call our own, and in only a year we did it.

We really could call it "our" home – because everyone in the family was contributing their paycheck! In only a few years, we were out of our third-level apartment and in a brand-new home we paid for together. As I recall, we paid about $17,000 for that house in late 1964 or early 1965. It was in North Leominster, Massachusetts, and it was brand new, the construction just finished. We would be the first people to live there! We doubled the space we had, going from a thousand square feet to about two-thousand square feet, meaning lots more comfort, lots more space, and a very welcome second bathroom.

We were here, and we were committed. America was now our home.

MCDONALD'S: THE START OF SOMETHING BIG (1967–1970)

Other than my relationship with my family, McDonald's is the biggest part of my life. It has been the main source of opportunity, satisfaction, and my education in business. It's not too much to say that everything good in my life that didn't start with my parents, my siblings, my wife, or my children began with McDonald's.

I believe in hard work. I believe that going to school has value, which is different from being smart, though both have a benefit – you can be born clever or you can study your way to get there. But let's not forget the role in life of plain, old luck. How did I end up at McDonald's?

There was a McDonald's restaurant close to my house. I needed a job, somebody had recommended I check it out, it was nearby, and that was that. Talk about good luck!

Another bit of my good luck with McDonald's came from bad luck somewhere else. Though McDonald's has been my "last" job, so to speak, it wasn't my first. Before that, I had worked a little in a plastics shop called Tucker Manufacturing, where my dad worked. I was 17 or so and they set me up as a handyman, which in this case was someone who would grind out bad plastic products into acceptable condition.

I got let go there.

The boss had asked me to clean out a room. Anything in there that was bad, I should toss in a truck and we'd haul it to the dump, those were my instructions. It turns out that one man's trash is another man's treasure, or in this case, vice versa. I decided that everything was bad. Instead of grinding any of it into something they could sell, I threw it all on the truck and sent it off to the scrap heap. When I was finished, that room was beautiful. It was also empty. This is not what they had in mind. The boss didn't agree with my (admittedly convenient) choice that pretty much everything was scrap. On that basis, they decided that I should seek employment elsewhere, or at least cease employment with them. That was the end of my days in manufacturing.

But I was lucky that happened because that freed me to go to my next job, the one that changed my life and the lives of so many others.

* * *

In 1967, when I was 17 years old, I started working at McDonald's Unit 466 in Fitchburg, Massachusetts. To put that unit number in perspective, there were at the time just under one thousand McDonald's restaurants in the country. Today, there are about 14,000 in the US and 38,000 around the world. McDonald's was still just a "kid" – and so was I.

I didn't know what my new job would lead to, but I knew that having this job was just the thing for a teenager with goals and dreams. It also turned out to be a great social advantage. Working with people in that environment helped me to become more comfortable in America. In addition, I could feel good about contributing to the family's income.

The restaurant was a great place to work. They were flexible with my work schedule. I think they liked me because anytime they needed someone to stay late or work another day, they would ask me and I would always say yes. I liked being there! The people who worked there were very pleasant, especially the management. It was hard work then, and it's hard work now, but that's true of any restaurant work. Still, I enjoyed it. I saw a future in it, too – perhaps not at first, but eventually.

I remember going in to work around 10:30 or 11:00 am to get ready for lunch because McDonald's didn't serve breakfast in those days. One of the main jobs to do before we opened was to prepare the French fries, and that began with peeling potatoes. We weren't doing that the way you might be picturing it. We weren't sitting over a bucket with a peeler, doing them one potato at a time, one slice at a time. We would put several potatoes in a container that had rough sides inside, like sandpaper. Then we flipped a switch to make it spin and that would peel the potatoes.

Next, we would pour the peeled potatoes into a stainless-steel sink, wash them thoroughly, then transfer them into yet another container, this one with blades to make fries. All you had to do was apply pressure, and the device would slice the potatoes into skinny fries, the same style still used by McDonald's today. Finally, we would wash them one more time and then pre-cook them – technically, we would blanch them, meaning we would boil them for a short time, then quickly cool them off to preserve their flavor, texture, and color.

With that, we had fries ready to cook, made fresh for that day and that day only. The next day, we'd do it all again.

There was other work, of course. That just happened to be the thing that took the longest each day, the thing with the most steps to follow. Whatever needed doing, that's what I would do, and what all of us would do. There was stocking to take care of, and sometimes major cleaning such as spraying down the sidewalks in front of the store, cleaning the restrooms, and scrubbing the floors. It was a worthwhile experience for any young person, and it taught me at an early age the value of discipline and hard work.

That was my first job with McDonald's. It made a huge impression on me, and it was my first connection in the most important professional relationship of my life.

* * *

In 1967, the menu at McDonald's was small but what we did, we did well. Having a small and simple menu was central to all that. Besides soft drinks and shakes, here's everything we offered:

- hamburgers,
- double hamburgers,
- cheeseburgers,
- double cheeseburgers,
- and French fries

That was it. We did only a few things, but we did them very well. There was much more to come, and I'm proud to say I was there for all of it, sometimes participating in the development and introduction of the product itself. So many things are a part of McDonald's now. We added apple pies, the Filet-o-Fish, the Quarter Pounder, and our breakfast menu, and those are just the best-known things – there were more, of course, though not everything stuck around. I could name menu items you never heard of that didn't last!

Eventually, we added the drive-thru, too, which of course changed everything for us and our customers and has since become a part of not just American culture but global culture.

In those days, McDonald's wasn't like it is today in terms of the physical layout. It was more of a hamburger stand, the kind the Beach Boys sang about in "Fun, Fun, Fun." There was no inside seating. You'd walk up to the counter. That meant if you worked there, you had a lot of contact with the customers, so it was important to be polite, to get the orders right, and to make people feel not just welcome but also happy to be there.

That wasn't difficult for me to do, because this restaurant was at the time a popular nighttime hangout for young people. So working there was a great social thing for me, a great way to see friends and make new ones, and of course, a great way to meet girls.

The experience of visiting McDonald's was first-rate, but the food was first-rate, too. Everything came from local suppliers, meaning the beef, the bread, the cheese, and the potatoes, and our suppliers would deliver the burgers to us already shaped into the patties per our standards. We were very careful with inventory because we wanted to serve the food as soon as possible and not pay for things that wouldn't sell and would have to be discarded. We put delicious, fresh food in front of our customers every day.

The restaurant business in those days was different than it would become in later years, different than it is today. Today, restaurants have a variety of dress codes and even uniforms for their employees, with some so casual that they don't have dress codes at all. But in those days, every restaurant of nearly every kind was strict – not formal but consistent, neat, and professional. Going out to eat was at some level an event. This was how it was everywhere. Even if a place was just a casual diner by the side of the road, you could almost always count on everyone who worked there dressing in a prescribed style every day. McDonald's was no exception. There was a particular smock you had to wear, and the store would provide one for you – more than one if you worked often enough. They would launder the jerseys, too, though I always took mine home because my mother did a better job and didn't mind doing it for me. You also had to have polishable shoes (black), a paper hat, and a hair restrainer or hairnet.

I think the best lesson to take from all that is this: when it comes to building a quality business, discipline, order, and quality are a lot more important than glamour.

I can't say enough good things about the quality of every part of the business. It impressed me then, and it impresses me now. The food was fresh and tasted good – still is and still does. That's easy to take for granted, but if you take it for granted, it won't be the best for long. If you're going to sell things to the public, it all begins with quality both in the product and in the experience.

* * *

In 1971, the restaurant owner sent me to McDonald's headquarters for two weeks of training. At the time, I was an assistant manager, but with this corporate education under my belt, I would come back to be promoted to general manager. This wasn't just any training program either. It's highly effective, and it's critical to anyone who wants to succeed in the McDonald's organization, which, thanks in part to its unusual name, is known around the world. In those days and still today, to become an owner-operator of a McDonald's, you have to go through a two-year process as a "registered applicant," and then the education process to learn the McDonald's system. You can also go through other parts of the process to become a manager or to add skills to your management ability.

To do any of those things means you have to graduate from "Hamburger University." The main classroom is not a classroom at all but a working McDonald's restaurant open to the public.

(I attended at the original location in Oak Brook, Illinois. Today, it's in the West Loop neighborhood of Chicago on the site of what were Oprah Winfrey's studios. The restaurant is open to the public so, yes, you can eat there – and you'll be served by the most hard-working professionals you'll ever meet.)

It was here that they made sure we understood and could act on McDonald's high standards and precise methods for food safety and quality control. You had to know a lot to graduate as a manager. If you were there to become an owner-operator, you had to learn even more. Either way, you were not allowed to graduate unless and until you could execute, every time, the proper procedures to make every sandwich and drink to an exacting standard. If you came through the program successfully, and not everyone did, you knew exactly what it takes to build a perfectly prepared hamburger, cheeseburger, and milkshake.

The McDonald's milkshake deserves special attention. Ray Kroc created the McDonald's we know today because he was selling multimixers in the mid-1950s. He met the McDonald brothers when he sold them those mixers for their restaurants. The rest, as they say, is history.

When I learned how to make a McDonald's milkshake, it was more an art than a science – often a very messy art. The main feature of the milkshake machine was a long spindle that turned at a high rate of speed, like an electric drill going at full blast, but with a twist. You would bring it down into the big cup of milkshake mix, keep it there until it reached the "just right" consistency and thickness, then you'd raise the spindle out. This sounds easy, but it wasn't. If you were in a McDonald's in those days more than once or twice, you had likely seen the messy evidence of this challenge, and it was all over some new crew member and his or her hapless colleagues. If you didn't carry out these seemingly simple moves exactly right, your half-made milkshake would go flying all over you and everybody else. Those "milkshake moves" had to happen faster than most people could react – well, faster than I could react, at least. It took me quite a while to get that job down.

Working, observing, and acquiring new skills at McDonald's was a great learning experience. In fact, the education I got at the restaurant was of far greater value than anything I got from high school or college. McDonald's was preparing me for the practicalities of life.

* * *

I think I was a pretty good worker in those days, but the thing that management liked most about me was that I was the most flexible worker they had. I was willing to take on any shift, any time. If you've ever worked in a business where staff has to be at a certain level every day, you know just how important flexibility is. You also know how difficult it can be to find people to fill in – which leads me to the following. As parents, we encourage our children by telling them that they are smart. That's a good thing to do, but time has taught me that something as important, if not more, is to compliment a young person on hard work. Being smart will take you pretty far, but unless it's matched with hard work, you won't be successful. Given the choice between someone who is smart and someone who is hard-working, I'll take the hard worker every time. One of the highest compliments you can pay me is to tell me I'm a hard worker. The people I admire most are first and foremost hard workers, people committed to getting the job done.

McDonald's was an ideal fit for me. It was then, and it still is. Early on, I thought I wanted to be a math teacher, but my studies would fall behind because I would rather stay at work and make money. It would break my mother's heart that I could close the restaurant at night and come home late, which made it hard for me to get up and go to school. This is not to say I didn't go. There were mornings when I was just too exhausted to go, but my mother would roll me out of bed and force me to go. Like most immigrant parents, especially in those days, my mother saw school as her son's ticket to a better life. But the truth is that sometimes, after working 40–45 hours a week, I would get in the car and go someplace where I could just sleep.

That's really what cemented that I wasn't going to be a teacher, but it seems to me that my life worked out pretty well anyway. I would make a career in the restaurant business. I was anxious to start making a living. I like to work. I liked it then. I like it now. I liked making money. I liked being appreciated. That's how I had seen my father succeed: on the strength of commitment and hard work. He could barely speak English, but his work ethic had been enough for him to support us very well and to navigate a world that was entirely new to him.

This is not to say all my brothers and sisters shared my outlook. They would succeed in other ways. For instance, my older brother went to school and became a plastics engineer. That's one of those careers that takes not only hard work but also high intelligence, and he has done well.

* * *

Something else happened in those years that I have to mention, something that would change my life, though I did not know it at the time. In fact, I didn't know about it until long after it happened.

In the late 1960s, I took some time away from my job at McDonald's to attend university full-time. While I was away in December 1969, a man named Richard "Rick" McCoy bought McDonald's #466, the restaurant where I had been working. The outlet had been wholly owned by McDonald's corporation. Now it had its own owner-operator, and he had ambitions to do even more: he would bring McDonald's to many communities in New England.

Mr. McCoy and his partner, Eugene "Gene" Colley, were two years into a partnership, the Colley/McCoy Company. Their goal was to build their own chain of McDonald's restaurants. This was an attractive opportunity for an entrepreneur – and a relatively new idea. Then as now, a McDonald's startup requires a significant investment, about $53,000 in 1969. By comparison, this is about five times the average household income at the time. But you got a lot of value for your investment, including the support of a thriving, youthful, positive brand with slick, national advertising and a system for establishing, running, and building a business that was already proven and in place at hundreds of locations. Unlike other businesses, you wouldn't have to feel your way by trial and error. If you were willing to work, McDonald's would show you the way.

Though franchising had existed in America since A&W Root Beer pioneered it in 1924, it wasn't until the 1950s that the model began to catch on with a few restaurant brands. From that perspective, Mr. McCoy and Mr. Colley were getting in if not on the ground floor then certainly the first or second story, and it was clear that McDonald's was going to be a skyscraper.

I returned from school, having decided that I didn't need a college education to reach the goals I had in mind. I presented myself at #466 hoping for my old job, and, sure enough, the new owners hired me back.

Mr. Colley ran the New York restaurants. Mr. McCoy ran the rest of New England. That meant he was the boss I saw the most, and his influence on my professional life – well, to describe it as "profound" would be a vast understatement. His was second only to the influence of my father. McCoy added immensely to my skills for business. He emphasized professionalism and imparted character.

I was fortunate that the people that I worked for, especially Mr. McCoy, cared about the future of the people who worked for him, especially the young people. Since he ran the day-to-day operation, he was right there with me, and his example was on display at all times. His influence was also felt in the quality management people he brought in because he made sure they were as engaged as deeply and as sincerely as he was. His commitment and vision helped many of us to make wonderful careers. I owe a debt of gratitude to Mr. McCoy for so much of what I believe today about character, honor, business, and life.

I didn't know it at the time, but in a few years, I would go from being one of their employees to being their business partner. Mr. McCoy would go from being my new boss to being a mentor and, ultimately, a friend. Decades later we would engage in a massive transaction that enabled him to retire from his spectacular career and enabled me to own, along with my son, one of the largest McDonald's chains in the United States.

But I'm getting ahead of myself.

BEGINNING A BLESSED FAMILY (1970–1971)

Throughout this book, I'll mention plenty of mountaintop moments – choices and achievements that changed my life for the better. But one beats them all.

It was easily the best decision I ever made: in December 1969, I decided to attend a house party. While I was there, I met Denise Champagne, the woman who would become my wife.

She is my closest friend, my partner in all things, and the love of my life.

In May 1971, less than two years after we met, we were married. We were very young to be married, though not so much for those days. Besides, we both knew what we wanted, so why wait? I was in a hurry to start making a real living, and from the moment I met her, Denise was my enthusiastic and loving partner.

We were and are very comfortable with one another, we enjoy each other's company, and we still look forward to every day together. As of this writing, we've been married 51 years. Since our wedding also marked when I went from part-time to full-time at McDonald's, that anniversary also marks how long I've been in this career. Make no mistake, we have stood together every step of the way, through the victories and the challenges. Denise has never wavered. If I felt something was the right thing to do, she would back me up. On occasion, as you'll soon read, those decisions put some of our finances into the mix, but, like me, she has always appreciated that reward and risk go hand in hand. Having her as my partner in our home life has always made my business life easier. Her confidence in me was no small part of the confidence I had in my judgment. I loved what I did, and I still do. I wanted to be good at it. She made that possible and made it into reality.

It's been a great run for Denise and me, and it continues to be, which is not to say it has always been easy for either of us or that it didn't take effort on both our parts. Between school and work, especially in the beginning, we didn't always have a lot of time together. She took the lead in raising our children, no question. Whatever time we managed to make together, though, became very, very important, and we made the most of it.

She may be the most understanding woman who ever walked the earth. I'm sure she's lost count of the number of times I've called to tell her I was ready to leave the restaurant, only to hear me coming in after midnight, having stayed to help the team anyway. A few more minutes too often turned to a few more hours and then to closing time more often than we can remember. There were as many reasons to have to stay late or change my plans with family as there are days in the year. Yet she was always supportive, always forgiving, always understanding.

I was not at home as much as I would have liked, nor as much as my wife and kids would have liked, either. Yet I'm proud to say that we still had a wonderful family life with many joyful times together and that she and I formed deep bonds that have held us together through the years and unite us still today.

* * *

Denise and I rented our first apartment in a building my dad owned. It was in a very depressed area, with some crime and some poverty, but we moved there because my father gave us a great deal. He remodeled the first-floor apartment for us at no cost, which was very generous and a gift in itself. But the best part, and the thing that made it an easy choice, was this: he charged us only $40 a month in rent. That would be unheard of today, but even in 1971, it was a great deal. We were very happy there.

I remember bringing Denise to meet my parents at their home, and I was pleased that I had a nice place to show her because she had grown up in a nice home herself. Her parents lived in a lovely French-Canadian neighborhood, 11th Street in Leominster, Massachusetts, in a house her father had built from scratch. He was quite handy and had done it the old-fashioned way: he bought the land, built the foundation, and put in the cellar, then he and his wife lived in the middle of all that while he finished constructing the house. My in-laws were a lovely couple, and I lucked out getting a great wife and her great parents as family as well. They were a great example: we were like-minded, modest, hard-working people.

Denise's father worked his entire life at Foster Grant, a sunglasses factory. Foster Grant was probably the biggest employer in Leominster with about 1,500 workers, if my memory serves. A lot of my family – distant cousins, uncles, and others – came to America from Pietraperzia and found work there. Denise's mom, a wonderful lady, worked her whole life as a beautician. She worked for a large firm called Henri's Hair Design, ultimately as a manager. Denise's folks worked hard and brought five children into the world. Her parents provided a wonderful life for their children and they shared a joyous family experience with me. I enjoyed spending time with them, especially Sunday dinner.

Unfortunately, they both became ill and passed relatively early. While only in her 60s, my mother-in-law was diagnosed with a severe case of Parkinson's disease. She had a tough time and died not long after – too young, I say – in her early 70s. My father-in-law also died sooner than he should have, after taking good care of his wife in her decline.

Denise and I lived in the apartment for quite some time – we had a plan – and after about two years, we were ready to take action.

For those two years, we focused on making money, keeping expenses to a minimum, and saving as much as we could. Denise began work as a secretary in a furniture factory, and this was our secret weapon. Every time she brought home a paycheck, we would deposit the whole thing in savings. It added up fast. Whenever we could "do without," we would. For instance, with both of us working, two cars would have been useful. Some would say they would even be a necessity. But we got by with one car because it was of course cheaper and would get us to our financial goal faster.

After we got married, I was promoted from assistant manager to manager – the result of my two weeks at Hamburger U. Denise and I would leave together for work. She would drop me off at McDonald's, then go to the furniture factory where she worked. At the end of the day, instead of going home, she would swing back by McDonald's and pick me up. I would drive her home and turn right around to get back to the restaurant so I could be there for the dinner rush, which is where the manager of a restaurant ought to be at that time.

Our sacrifice and planning worked. By about 1973, we had saved enough for our down payment. With a little guidance from my brother, Joe, who was in the real-estate business, we bought a brand-new home, a split-entry in Ashburnham, Massachusetts, that listed for $37,000. To put that in perspective, the average home price in America at that time was just below $27,000, and the average family income was a little over $12,000. Prices and wages have shifted considerably since then, plus there's inflation to consider and the higher cost of living where we were living at the time, but I share this for a reason: I want to emphasize how proud I am of what Denise and I did together to establish a life for ourselves and our family; only a few years out of our teens, we secured a home quickly.

(As a fun aside, there's this. With that first home, we established a little rule – a treat for ourselves. We decided that any home we ever purchased would have to have a fireplace. If it didn't have one, I'd put one in – and I did so on at least one occasion, years later.)

Things became a little more challenging after our son was born. Denise continued to work but shifted to part-time to take care of the baby. We had to keep being careful with money. For instance, I remember waiting until the last minute to pay our mortgage so the check wouldn't bounce. Fortunately, we were never late – at least, as far as I can recall now. We would wait until the last minute to buy most things – we were watching every cent.

* * *

Our children are all wonderful people, and Denise and I are blessed to have them in our lives.

Our oldest is Sal. We named him Salvatore after my father, which is the Sicilian tradition. Denise was kind enough to consent to this. She had a great deal of love and respect for my parents and was happy to be a part of our custom and to do something that made me so proud and my father, especially. As far as I'm concerned, my father was the smartest and the best, though I know many of us feel that way about our fathers – and we are certainly entitled to feel that way! I am proud that my father demonstrated his wisdom and caring throughout his life. If there was any hesitation it was from naming a little child *Salvatore*, an Italian name, in the United States – not as common as Mike, Jim, or even Tony. But Sal has done pretty well with the family name, if I do say so myself.

He married his high-school sweetheart, Sabrina, and they've been married for over 20 years. She's a lovely person and Denise and I consider her a daughter, and we love that she's a wonderful mother to their children, Peter, in his second year of college as I write this, and Sophia, in her second year of high school.

Today, Sal is one of the leaders of our company. He came aboard in 1994 when we were still in partnership with Mr. McCoy, and he followed the path I require of anyone who wants to move up with us. He has a degree from Northeastern University, and he's my oldest child, but as I've made clear here, none of those things are substitutes for learning the business by doing it. Sal started as a team member, learning the stations and tasks behind the counter, opening the restaurant and closing it, learning food preparation, service, and cleanup – you name it, he did it, and just the same as anyone else who aspires to be a part of our organization.

I remember that, not long after he started, my cousin Piero came to visit us from Italy, and we went to see Sal working at the restaurant. There he was, behind the counter – much to Piero's surprise.

"Pete," he said, "why does he have to work like that? He's your son."

You already know what I said. "Well, Piero, how else is he going to know how to teach and direct crew members when he becomes a manager?"

I'm very fortunate that Sal enjoys the work as much as I do, but the best thing is that he's exceptionally good at it. (Though I don't want him to get a swelled head, he's better at all this than I am.) He learned the business from the ground up, he cut no corners, and he didn't once ask me to make an exception for him because he is family. Mr. McCoy was very gracious in allowing me as a minority partner to bring my son into the business and teach him the business. When the time was right, we made him an area supervisor and later our operations manager – not because he was my son but because he had worked his way up the ladder, proven himself at every turn, and shown his value to our operation.

When we bought out Mr. McCoy in 2003, Sal became a partner with me. He's a great son, a great partner, and a great leader.

* * *

Our second child was a daughter, Cettina, or Tina for short. We named her that because my mother had no opportunity to name a child after her mother. We thought this was the perfect opportunity to fill the gap and honor a wonderful woman.

Tina has a lot of ambition. She worked for us at McDonald's a little bit when she was in high school, but she figured out pretty quickly that the restaurant business wasn't for her. That said, she was a hard worker who was glad to have the job because she wanted to have some money of her own; and when you're talking about teenagers, that's a pretty strong motivation to do a good job.

She attended Northeastern University and upon graduation became a dental hygienist in Boston. She made an impressive living at it, too – far more than I was earning at that age! She was very successful living on her own. Unlike her parents, she didn't marry young. She wanted to be by herself and independent, which we certainly respected.

She didn't need help from her mom and dad, but if you've ever been a parent, you know it's hard for parents to keep their distance. For instance, there was her purchase of a condominium. She could have handled the whole thing by herself, but she didn't object when Denise and I coached her a bit through the process – at least she let us offer our advice. When the sale was worked out, we joined her at the closing. If you've ever attended a real-estate closing, you know what goes on. It's a big event in terms of what it means to your finances, but that importance is wholly out of proportion to the little meeting because not much happens.

We arrived at the closing in a triumphant mood. Tina had the guts to make this purchase, and she knew it was a wise move financially, but when the moment arrived and the deal was completed, the reality of the situation hit home. She had just been through the process of signing all these papers, seemingly hundreds of pages of attorney mumbo-jumbo, and finally, the deed was done. It gave way to a funny, sweet moment as we walked out.

Through tears, she said, "How am I gonna pay this monthly mortgage?"

She could make the payments, and of course, she knew it was the right thing to do, the smart play for a young woman building a future. But no matter how prepared you are, the first time you sign those kinds of papers, reality strikes.

Of course, her trepidation faded fast, and a year or two later, she was ready to move up to a larger place and, of course, she did – and she negotiated and closed that deal with far more confidence, and all by herself.

Not long after, while attending a wedding, she ran into Jack. They had known each other for many years through Jack's sister but had never gotten acquainted. Not long after that wedding, there was another: they were married. Denise and I are blessed to have

Jack in our lives. He is like a son to us. These days, he's quite a successful business owner-operator. His holdings include several cleaning businesses, plus an operation that provides repair for restaurant equipment and facility maintenance and construction. Not long after Tina and Jack met, they moved to Arlington, Massachusetts, and today they're the parents of Jake, Chloe, and, more recently, Hazel, whom they adopted from Ethiopia – and on that hangs a tale.

Around 2018, life was pretty busy for Jack and Tina. Tina had recently purchased a children's boutique, a fixture in the community since 1938. This kept her quite occupied, but things were about to get busier. She had met some people who had adopted children from Ethiopia, and she decided that she wanted to help a child in this way herself. In the best tradition of our family, she kept all those balls in the air. She had her mind made up, and she did what she set out to do.

She described the orphanage in a way that tugs at your heart, with a room full of cribs where babies stay nearly every hour of the day. Who couldn't be moved by that? Jack and Tina made the trip to meet Hazel and bring her home, and they anticipated being gone for about ten days. Denise and I took on the babysitting for Jake and Chloe, and I have to tell you that I had forgotten how demanding even very well-behaved children can be for that length of time! There's a line in a movie that occurs to me, and I'll clean it up a little here: *I'm getting too old for this stuff.* But I have to say that I was delightfully exhausted at the end of each day, getting to spend so much quality time with these grandchildren of ours and knowing that Jack and Tina would be back soon with the newest member of our family.

They had all kinds of difficulty getting the appropriate paperwork, so much so that the 10-day trip stretched into three weeks. But when they returned in what by then was February, it was a wonderful, wondrous, emotional reunion for us all.

The arrival of our latest grandchild struck me as an occasion for a special celebration and perhaps an opportunity to show off my beautiful family. We had a McDonald's convention approaching in less than two months, and I declared that we would go to this event as a family, every one of the 15 of us in attendance.

I try not to brag, and I hope this doesn't sound like a boast – well, it is a boast, if I'm being honest, but it's not a boast about material wealth. It's an expression of the pride I felt in being able to enjoy the fruits of my labor as a businessman, to appreciate my wife as the person who looked after our family and raised our children so well, and to take joy from spending time with my children and grandchildren, whose character and achievements make me proud and make the world a better place. So, in that sense? Sure, I'm bragging. I wanted this to be a special trip, one for the ages, one we would always remember on the occasion of Hazel's arrival.

We set out for Florida, the whole lot of us, by private jet – not my usual way of travel, I can assure you, but this was no usual trip. We stayed at the Four Seasons and enjoyed everything they had to offer. I remember sitting in one of our rooms at that magnificent hotel, looking over my precious new granddaughter, Hazel, and thinking about the life she left behind compared to the opportunities my daughter and son-in-law would make for her. It was a joyous occasion.

* * *

Last – but, as they say, certainly not least – I'd like to introduce our youngest daughter, Melissa. After the first two names came from my side of the family, it was well past time for the woman who carried all three of them to do the honors, and Denise chose that beautiful name.

Melissa was, as the saying goes, a surprise – a bonus baby. To the extent that Catholic parents can plan such things, Denise and I had decided to have only two children, and they were five years apart. But another five years passed and we encountered this wonderful surprise in the form of a third child. I'm tempted to ask what I asked at the time, *how does this happen?* But the answer always makes me laugh, as it does most people who experience this kind of blessing: it happens!

It wasn't what we planned, but some of the best things in life are surprises, and this definitely falls into that category. Five years after our last child, our professional and financial situations were considerably different. We were established, so we could afford this – in fact, the thought we had was *the more, the merrier.* Melissa's arrival was a great gift and a true joy.

Like her brother and sister, Melissa is ambitious and successful. Unlike them, she never worked at McDonald's, which is to this day the source of some teasing. She chose her own path, coming only a few years behind them at the Catholic school in Fitchburg, starting with St. Bernard's Elementary on Summer Street, then St. Bernard's High School on Harvard Street. Like her siblings, Melissa went to Northeastern where she earned her master's degree in education. She of course became a teacher, and that makes me especially proud because teachers molded my life in important ways, from learning English to helping me understand America and fit in, thus paving the way for me to have the life I've enjoyed. Teachers are vital, so when Melissa decided that she wanted this career, I was overjoyed.

Her first job was at a Catholic elementary school in East Boston where she taught second grade. She said that the interview was memorable in that the roles were somewhat reversed. Usually, it's the person applying for the job who's in need, not the other way around. "We're happy to give you a job as a teacher," the interviewer said. "We can't pay the kind of wage I know you'd want, but we can provide a lot of love." And that, they did. Melissa took the job and gained a great deal of experience – there's that word again – that would serve her well in the years to come, and she told me that she got a kick out of the first time in front of her own classroom. At the time, the Napoli Group owned the McDonald's not far from the school, so we had a fundraiser to donate a portion of the day's sales to the school.

Melissa taught there for a few years and then was fortunate enough to sign on as a second-grade teacher in Leominster, nearer to where she grew up. She taught there for several more years and met her husband. Dennis Kohut is a wonderful man, like a son to us, and he does us all proud because he earned his own master's degree and has spent time as both a high-school English teacher and principal. After a decade of teaching, Melissa took time off to start their family, and she's been happily busy as a full-time parent ever since, looking after the household and caring for their two boys, Nolan, who is nine, and Colin, who is six.

* * *

Everyone has to make their own path. Of our 13 children and grandchildren, some have already made it pretty far, some are just starting out, and some are beginning to make their marks, but all of them make us proud. Denise and I look forward to the accomplishments that we know lie ahead for them. These young people are the greatest legacy she and I could have.

And that brings me back to where this chapter began: with the woman who started it all.

When we were young parents, Denise worked as hard as I did, probably harder. At least I got to leave the job at the end of the day. She was on call 24/7! I was working six- and even seven-day weeks, making her the primary caregiver for our children, and often the only one there. She took care of schooling and handled discipline. She managed the household – and when five people live there all the time, there's more in common with managing a restaurant than you might think. On top of all that, she worked part-time and brought in income.

Call it a division of labor – we both did our part, but I deeply appreciate what she did, dedicating her life to making a home for our family. She was amazing then, and she is amazing today. She assumed great responsibility and did it with a smile and with kindness for all of us.

Thanks, Denise. I love you.

THE RIGHT THING REGARDLESS (1971–1973)

The Colley/McCoy Company started in 1967 with two restaurants. It was growing quickly, and that would create opportunities for me. It would also provide a moment of validation – a lesson, really – in the value of doing the right thing.

In 1971, when I was first made a manager, the group had grown to 7 restaurants. The next year, we were up to 17 restaurants, more than doubling the holdings. In 1973, we reached 23, more than 300 percent growth in less than 3 years. When you're opening a new restaurant every 30 to 60 days, you're looking at an all-hands-on-deck situation. I had prepared myself to be useful in such a situation. Now they needed committed, responsible people to oversee the restaurants already in place and execute more growth. They chose me.

So in 1973, Mr. McCoy promoted me to area supervisor. He told me that he liked my work, my choice of hires, the way I had built up customer satisfaction, and of course that I had maintained and added to sales and profit.

"Do what you're doing here," he said, "but in four restaurants."

Instead of running a single location, I would now oversee four McDonald's restaurants: Brattleboro, Vermont; Keene, New Hampshire; Leominster, Massachusetts; and Fitchburg, Massachusetts. Over the years, each place would come to have a special meaning to me. I started with the company in the Fitchburg restaurant, and Denise and I would raise our family in Leominster. At various times, I would own all four of those restaurants – Brattleboro and Keene I still own.

One of the things I had done that Mr. McCoy liked was something I learned from him. I would arrive at the restaurant, take out a piece of paper, then fold it over and put it in my pocket with a pencil. I would tour every corner of the restaurant, asking questions of the people who were working that day, and write down whatever I saw that could be done better or easier. Whether it was how somebody was doing a job, a piece of equipment that needed attention, or some issue with the taste or quality of the food, I would take out my paper and pencil and make a note. Then I would sit down with the manager and go through the list, giving them specific guidance about what needed to be done, how it needed to be done, and what and when I expected it to be done. In addition, I would mention the things I saw that were exemplary – there were always many – and compliment and encourage them for their excellent work.

It's a simple method, but sometimes the simple way is the best. It helped improve my first restaurant and kept it running smoothly. Now it had helped me get a big promotion. In terms of responsibility, it was a big move up. I thought I was ready, and I was excited to have earned it. I would be making many more decisions than before. That included deciding how much people got paid.

Not long after I started, Mr. McCoy summoned me to his office just up the road in Salem, New Hampshire. I didn't know why he had called me but of course, I came right away. Maybe he wanted to congratulate me on my good work!

After the usual small talk, he asked me if I had been looking in on the payroll every week. I wasn't sure what he was getting at, since payroll is something you set up or change as needed and then monitor to make sure it's going out appropriately. There aren't a lot of moving parts.

"Yes, sir," I said. "I keep an eye on it, of course."

"I keep an eye on it, too," he said, "and I noticed that you have a maintenance man who just got a big raise."

It was true. I had given him an outsized raise and for good reason. Billy was – well, the word is *magnificent*. For one thing, he kept the restaurant spotless. For another, he could do just about anything, and with minimal instruction. I had wanted to build a crew room in the basement and had set him to work on the project. I hadn't had to do much more than say the word. I bought the lumber, and he quickly had it done. When Billy figured out how valuable he was to the restaurant, he threatened to leave, but the threat was almost surely a tactic to get a raise – and a raise he deserved, I must say. Mr. McCoy had empowered me to make such a decision, and I did. I gave Billy the raise, gratefully. It reflected his value.

"Did you know," said Mr. McCoy, "that, some weeks, the maintenance guy makes more than you do?"

Well, no. I had not known that.

"I never really paid attention to that comparison," I said. "But instead of comparing his paycheck to mine, let me explain why his check is what it is," I told Mr. McCoy what Billy did daily, the special project he had recently completed, and the value Mr. McCoy's restaurant enjoyed from having someone on call with his skills. Mr. McCoy accepted my justification. He had shown confidence in me when he gave me the job in the first place. He trusted my judgment. At that moment, when I needed to explain my choices, he liked what I had to say.

Put another way, his judgment about my judgment turned out to be good judgment.

"Good enough, Peter," he said. "But be careful, okay?"

I had been careful, but it was good to know it was appreciated. Plus the exchange provided an additional lesson: if you do the right thing in business, you may have to explain it, but you'll never have to apologize for it. Allowing this maintenance person to do his job properly and take on more responsibility was good for the operation, so it made sense that I should pay him more. He was delivering value to our company in exchange for the money we paid him.

Put in more direct terms, we were engaging in a profitable exchange. We were purchasing something that had value to us, something that helped us continue to do business and make a profit better than we could without it.

* * *

Doing the right thing always matters.

Not long ago, I was at the home of my daughter, Melissa, and we decided to order pizza from a place called Dino's in nearby Concord. It was the second time that week I'd been in a pizza joint, but the experiences were far different.

A few days earlier, in a restaurant whose name I won't mention, the place was obviously short on staff. The dining room wasn't open, and they had limited hours. You could tell they were struggling. But only a few miles away, Dino's was busy! This place had a dozen people working that I could see, maybe more.

What accounts for such a difference? A comfortable environment for the employees, paying the people well, and creating opportunities they can take advantage of to get ahead are the three things I know are vital to attracting and keeping employees as part of a successful business. Everyone there was engaged with the task at hand, they made me feel welcome, and they radiated the feeling that they were happy to be there – and happy to have me there, too.

I was particularly impressed by this: when I arrived at Dino's, I gave them my name for the order, paid the bill, and gave a tip to the woman behind the counter. Because the place was so busy, I decided to go outside and wait there for my order. A few minutes later, the young lady who had been behind the counter came out with my pizza. She hadn't called my name and just set it aside. She took it upon herself to remember where I had gone, to carry my order out of the restaurant, and to put it in my hands. That's service that makes a difference, so much so that I'm telling you about it in my book.

If that lady wasn't the owner, I guarantee that she can be. She already gets it. Success belongs to those who hustle, and that means going the extra mile in terms of customer care and old-fashioned courtesy. When you do more than you have to, whether that's as a worker or an employer, you're doing the right thing and the smart thing, and it's the surest path to plenty.

A good way to keep yourself in that mindset is to think of where you work not as "their" place but as "ours" and "mine." If you go back to the start of this section, you'll notice that when I write about my employer at the time, the Colley/McCoy Company, I talk about "our" growth and "our restaurants." At that time they weren't "my" restaurants at all.

But I conducted myself as if they were. That has made all the difference.

* * *

As an employer, how do you encourage people to think this way? You make them a part of what you do and remind them of their value to you. In short, you treat them like family.

As I write this book, we're living in a time when there are lots of jobs and lots of people to fill them but little incentive to work – perhaps the pay is too low compared to the requirements, or for some, they are getting their bills paid by other people or in other ways. Whatever the reason, the problem of coming up short-staffed remains, and it's up to employers to incentivize a workforce. Getting people to work for us has never been a problem for the Napoli Group. That's because of three things:

1) we have a comfortable environment where people enjoy working,

2) we pay our people well, especially in terms of the skills they bring to the job and the benefit they bring to our workplace, and

3) we create wonderful growth opportunities that anyone can take advantage of, anytime, if that's what they would like to do.

It's another case of doing the right thing. The right thing to do is usually the smart thing to do. In this case, success breeds success, and a rising tide lifts all boats.

* * *

When I think back on those early days of my professional life at McDonald's, I return over and over to the positive attitude I saw from management and the executive office toward the people who worked there. This early encounter with the power of doing the right thing had benefits for me, too, but I made the right choice in part because others had set this powerful, positive example in the years before.

When I was starting out, folks who ran McDonald's at every level were always looking for good people. It's still that way today, except now I'm one of the people looking for those exceptional candidates – and now I know why. Having a good head for business is having a good head for people – appreciating what they do best and what they enjoy, identifying what characteristics they have that will help the business, and being able to leverage their excellence to build excellence in others.

It's not just about growing the business: it's also about helping people find excellence in themselves.

If you're a dedicated, ambitious person who wants to work, call me. We can always use someone interested in working with us, growing with us, and working hard. Our consistent growth allows us to keep hiring. We like to get 'em young, probably because it's always in the back of my mind that there's someone out there like me who will start with McDonald's as a teenager or young adult and find the same satisfaction, and even joy, that I've found over the years. (That's probably why I take so much pleasure in training. There's a lot of satisfaction in helping people do their best.)

Young people like to work in the restaurant atmosphere and tend to do well there. As one of those young people in the 1960s, I started at the McDonald's in Fitchburg, Massachusetts, near my house. It wasn't close enough to walk to, but by this time I had a car of my own: a Ford Falcon. Not bad for a 17-year-old boy, though there was one drawback: I can say with complete confidence that the Ford Falcon was one of the ugliest cars ever made. My parents had helped me buy it, and I was grateful to have it but not so attached to it that I didn't trade up as soon as I could for a late-model Mustang.

A young boy with a job and a Mustang: to say that out loud – and to think about what that meant in the 1960s and 1970s – conjures up an image of happiness, satisfaction, and fun. My son, Sal, and I talk about this often: when it comes to our ownership of McDonald's restaurants, the most important thing we can do to grow our business and benefit our employees is to create a comfortable and fun atmosphere. People who are happy do better work; plus, I feel I owe it to them to create a work environment that's not just pleasant but also makes them look forward to being there.

Of course, you have to pay them well, too. I am fortunate to have been on the receiving end of that outlook, and it has greatly influenced how I do things now that I'm the one signing the checks. When I started out, jobs were a little scarcer than they are today, so there were opportunities for employers to get away with paying less than perhaps they should have. But the way I remember it, I felt that I was being paid well and fairly. Maybe I didn't know any better, but that's the way I remember it. It was a fair trade for my youthful labor.

When I felt I wasn't earning what I deserved, I would ask for a raise, which I always got. I wouldn't ask for more just because time had passed or because I thought they were prime for hearing my appeal. When I thought I deserved more for what I contributed, I asked for more, and they always agreed.

* * *

The restaurant business really has been the best business for me. It has been rewarding in so many ways, starting with how impressive it is that so much gets done so well and so quickly! Our people meet a consistently high standard every day. The average McDonald's serves 1,000–1,500 customers a day, some even more. It's rewarding to be a part of making that happen, from the days when I was on the crew all the way up to now, where my job is all about planning and execution.

When I consider the successful people I know, I always find that they cultivated success, hard work, and commitment in everyone they met. This is certainly the case in the restaurant business. When the person at the top is invested in the success of everyone else, not only do you build excellence in terms of food, service, and environment but you end up with those enthusiastic people building great careers and making their lives happier and more satisfying. The benefits of that ripple out.

LEARNING BUSINESS BY DOING BUSINESS (1973–1975)

As an area supervisor, my new responsibilities also included opening our new restaurants. Those three little words, "opening a restaurant," represent more work than you might imagine.

The first opening I was assigned came in 1974 with the Brattleboro, Vermont, operation. I was there literally night and day, taking time away only occasionally to grab a few hours of sleep in a nearby hotel. With a new restaurant, there's a lot on the line. I knew that it was vital for me to get things right.

One afternoon, while all this preparation was going on, Mr. McCoy came by. He understood how demanding these openings are, and he told me things were looking good. I was glad to get his approval because he had seen plenty of these openings and knew instinctively when something was off.

"Looking good, Pete," he said. "What do you say we go grab a bite of dinner?"

"I'm sorry, Mr. McCoy," I said. "I can't leave. I have to stay here and make sure it's all going right."

I turned down my boss for a one-on-one dinner.

At first blush, that may not sound like a wise move, but it was the only correct answer. I showed him where my priorities lay and that this business mattered perhaps as much to me as it did to him.

Surely a couple of hours wouldn't hurt, you say?

But it would have hurt. I knew that not because I was an area supervisor. I knew because I had been a crew member and manager – I knew how that restaurant operated from stem to stern.

My experience working every job told me that, on this particular evening, our Brattleboro restaurant wouldn't delight our customers if it lost not only my direction but also my pair of hands.

* * *

It was a good early lesson I was putting to use. Leaders need an understanding of business principles, for sure. But leaders also need to know the nitty-gritty of the business they are in.

If you don't understand every aspect of what your people do each day, you're not equipped to lead – and not equipped to make the right decisions when a choice has to be made. There are no exceptions.

A qualified leader knows every job. In our case, that means knowing firsthand what it means to work on a crew in a McDonald's, to meet the customers face to face, and to have the experience of what it's like to have your work affect customers the second you do it. The only way to get quality in those things, day in and day out, is commitment. In our business, demonstrating commitment takes the form of knowing a lot of things and doing them well: food safety, food preparation, cleanliness, and courteous service to the customers who have chosen to come to our restaurant. When I was a restaurant manager, that was my mission, to show everyone who worked for me how to do their job and do it well. This not only gave me great satisfaction with my work – it also gave me great satisfaction in demonstrating character. I got to set them on their way in their career, whether it would be with us or somewhere else. I took great pride in developing these young people, and I still do.

Of course, that attitude has always been at the heart of our company. Look at the results.

* * *

Everyone in senior positions in our company started in the restaurants. Come to our headquarters in Amherst, New Hampshire, open the door to any office, and you'll find someone who's done it all, starting with working in the kitchen or behind the counter. Jeremy Hinton is our president. He started as a crew member while attending high school and then college at the University of New Hampshire. When he graduated, he stayed with us as a manager, which is pretty much the same career path as my own. He then rose to supervisor, operations manager, and vice president, and now he is the president and director of operations of our company. He has been with us for 31 years. I want to help people build careers, so I have made my priority a priority of the entire operation, and it brings me great pleasure to see people succeed. It's the thing that I have enjoyed most.

Another great example is the wonderful Lynne Shields, who started with us in Leominster while she was still in high school. Later, she showed interest in what we do in the office, so when one of the supervisors needed some support, we found a place for her there. When I needed somebody in my office, we moved her into that job. Through that, she learned the business. You'll notice that when I talk about people finding – or seeking¬ – success in our organization, I look for commitment, hard work, and a willingness to do what needs to be done. Education is a good thing, but that's not the first thing I look for. We evaluate people based on what they show us they can do. I'm not very interested in what degree you have or even if you went to college. Just show me you belong here, you share our values, and you are willing to learn how to do the job.

Lynne is such a great example of the power of commitment. For many years, her job was to take over things I used to do, such as certain human resources tasks and a few matters of management and supervision. But the bottom line is that, like everyone else here, she does whatever needs to be done. She's been with us for 39 years, and today she's our vice president.

You won't find too many businesses where people turn a career into a lifetime, let alone an organization where the philosophy of the company is to make that possible for anyone who wants it. You certainly don't find this kind of longevity in the restaurant business. So if I sound proud, it's because I am.

* * *

This intense period of a couple of years convinced me of a truth I have called on daily ever since: the best way to learn is by doing.

As an area supervisor, part of my responsibility was to do the hiring for management positions in the McDonald's restaurants I oversaw. In nearly every case, the people we would hire for these jobs came from inside the organization, usually having started working as a member of the crew, just as I did when I was a teenager.

Education is good for a lot of things, but managers have to do more than a textbook education. They – we – have to know how things work by having done every job. You can't read a book or listen to a talk and really appreciate, heart and soul, what goes on when you work as a member of the crew. I've sat across from lots of people with far more education than I have who didn't understand the practical nature of the work they'd be supervising before taking on a position in management.

I remember a conversation from those days with a job seeker. He was a very good person, a very nice person, which I mention because the outcome of this encounter had nothing to do with how nice he was. This person's credential was their college education, which was well earned, I'm sure. "I have this degree," they told me. "I want to work for you, but, at the very least, I want to come in as a restaurant manager. Honestly, I'd like to come in at your level, doing your job."

There's an old saying that applies here: you may be the sweetest peach on the tree, but not everybody is looking for a peach.

"Do you think you could do the manager's job?" I said. "Could you go in right now and teach new crew members how to prepare food? Could you order our supplies? How about food safety? You can read the rules and regulations, but do you know how they work in practice? Can you care for our equipment? If you took over my job, you'd be hiring people. What are the skills you're looking for? What do new employees need to know? What can they do without? What can you teach them? And how will you motivate them – have you thought about that?"

This young man quickly understood that while education is valuable, experience matters as well, and one is no substitute for the other. I offered to bring him on and even pay him a little more as a nod to his education, but there was no wavering on the main point: he had to learn the business from the ground up. That meant spending time as a crew member, learning everything from how to prepare the food to how to clean up and close the restaurant at night.

"I've already interviewed with the competition," he said. "No offense, but they're willing to hire me, too. And they'll start me out in management."

"I'm going to make a prediction," I said. "You'll take that job, and in a few months or weeks you're going to quit."

"How do you figure that?" he said. "You think I'm not smart?"

"Just the opposite," I said. "You're plenty smart. You're so smart, in fact, that you're going to figure out something very important, very soon."

"Which is…," he asked.

"That your success isn't just about how hard you work, how much you've studied, or how much you want to succeed. You're going to figure out that in this business, there's no substitute for experience."

It is the same today: we look inside for people who have done all the jobs they will be supervising. There's a lot of wisdom that comes from that kind of experience. I speak with people in the restaurant business beyond McDonald's, and they're always surprised. I don't know why. All you have to do is take a look at the success that has come from doing it this way and the advantage is obvious.

I'm glad I learned it early!

LESSONS FROM A LANDLORD (1975–1981)

When I was in my early 20s working as an area supervisor, my brother Joe was in the real estate business. Like him and so many others in my family, I too decided to get into real estate. I wanted additional income and to start building equity for whatever opportunities might appear. I began to purchase apartments, starting with small, multi-family dwellings, because I had lived in those kinds of places myself.

I told my tenants, "I'm in the restaurant business, not the rental business. I have a full-time job. When you have a problem, I can't come over and fix it, so I'll have to pay someone to do it. So call when you have a problem, but whatever you can do on your own is going to save both of us time and trouble. That means the more you call, the more the rent goes up. It's really that simple."

You may think that's being harsh, but it's also being honest. They enjoyed a low-end-of-the-market rental price because they agreed to be more judicious than other renters might be. Did their rent include reasonable maintenance? Of course. But I couldn't be at their beck and call. In exchange, they saved some money. It turned out to be a good way to run my real-estate business. Tenants stayed with me because I was reasonable and transparent.

Before I was thirty, my holdings reached 19 units and became the key to capitalizing (literally) on an opportunity that would come my way years down the road. At the time, though, it had other benefits – and not only income. My favorite was that it led to a fruitful and delightful relationship with my friend and colleague, John.

* * *

From the start, John was the glue of the operation. I'd pick up the rent checks personally, making the stops on my way to or from work. It was much more secure than having people mail it in. (I know how that works: *the check's in the mail!* We've all heard that. Some of us have said that, too.) But when I couldn't be there, John was.

I equipped my rental units with a refrigerator and a stove. If a tenant had a problem with the appliances or anything else, I'd call John. When he could fix it, he fixed it, and when he couldn't, he'd haul off the old refrigerator or stove or whatever it was and sell me a used one at a good price from his sideline in used appliances. In this way, we both benefited regularly, and it never took more than a phone call.

In fact, our relationship was conducted entirely on the phone. He was a friend but only a voice. I relied on the guy, but I couldn't have picked him out of a lineup.

Fast forward to the early 1990s, almost two decades later. We were about to build the second McDonald's I would own, the one in Townsend, Massachusetts. I had gone to a public hearing to seek approval for the new construction. Some people were there opposing it. They argued, in so many words, that their community was "too good" for a McDonald's – though I could never understand how people who claim to want the best for others could oppose a multi-million-dollar business that creates starter jobs, part-time jobs, full-time employment, and management opportunities for dozens of their fellow citizens. After they had read off their list of grievances, it was my turn.

"Here's my phone number," I said, and I read the digits slowly aloud. I wanted them to write this down. "If you see litter, you call me at home, and I'll personally come down and pick it up," I said. I followed that with a point-by-point account of how I would deal with their concerns, the benefits we had brought to other, similar communities nearby, and what we intended to do here. Did my little speech convince them? I'll never know because of what happened next.

A young man stood up, someone I had never seen in my life. "I know Peter Napoli," he said.

"Who in the world is this guy?" I thought. I couldn't imagine who would say such a thing when clearly it wasn't true.

"If he says you can call him if there's a problem, you can call him," he said. Now he had their attention. "He'll take care of it. That's what I've seen him do my entire life. I'm a local business owner, myself. You know me, and I'm vouching for him."

I'll never forget my next thought: *this must be John.* We hadn't met! It had all been on the phone! And here he was – *so that's what he looks like!* – a well-respected local business owner standing up for me at a meeting in his own town and saving the day. He was the best pal I'd never met.

It occurred to me that we hadn't even been doing business all those years on a handshake. We'd done it on word and deed. It was a gratifying feeling.

* * *

When you're a landlord, you get a good look at what you otherwise would know only from personal experience. If your job is to collect rent, you sometimes see what the rest of the world does when they're in a tight spot. Conflict reveals character.

When I had an open apartment, I'd show the place personally. Once, I rented to a young man near my age who was dealing with an alcohol problem. He and his girlfriend needed a place. I immediately realized that I knew him. He was not going to be a reliable tenant, but I wanted to help. It wasn't a no-risk proposition for me. I still had to make the mortgage on the property, and I might have to make it some months without the rental payment, but I let him sign the lease anyway. I was pleased to be able to help, but I was also concerned about the liability.

For a while he could pay, but then the alcohol problem grew, and he couldn't often make the rent. Once, the phone rang on Christmas Eve. Denise answered. "Tell Peter not to get too excited by the call," he said. "I don't have the rent. I just wanted to wish you Merry Christmas." We chatted a bit, exchanging greetings and talking about the holiday. It was cordial, but cordiality wasn't the problem. It was the drinking.

A few months later, with no real change having been made,

my attitude became "in for a penny, in for a pound." I called Andy, our landscaper, and asked him to give our tenant a break by providing some employment – but, more importantly, by providing some guidance on how to improve his life by helping him to keep this job.

"He's in a bad way," I said, "but there's an opportunity here for him. Take him on. Kick him in the ass a little. Let's see what he does." My tenant had worked for a landscaper before, so it wasn't an entirely new experience. But having someone give him a hand at this low point was important.

Andy was happy to help. He provided an opportunity for my tenant, and I'm pleased to tell you that the job worked out. Regular work and encouragement – and discipline – helped my tenant pay most of the back rent and get his life more on track. It wasn't a perfect ending. He still disappeared once in a while, but our little arrangement made things better for both of us.

* * *

I never hired an attorney to help me with problem tenants. A lawyer can get someone out of your property, but you can usually finesse things to get the same outcome without writing a check for the privilege. Throughout the years that I owned apartments, I didn't lose any significant money on "bad" tenants. When you have a problem collecting, sometimes it takes a carrot, sometimes a stick. Though occasionally neither one works.

Denise had been working as a secretary in a hospital emergency room when she had an experience like the one I had had a few months before: she met someone who needed both an apartment and a break. The woman didn't have the deposit and the monthly rate was out of her price range, but we did want to help, so we changed the terms and got her moved in. Our new tenant was an exceptionally kind person and a single parent. She wouldn't turn out to be a problem at all.

The issue would be her kids.

This nice lady was a mother to two teenagers who were beyond her control. As soon as the three moved in, the kids made the place a community party pad. There was traffic in and out at all hours, they were destroying the place, and they made so much noise that the other tenants were calling to complain. (How bad was it? One call came from the fellow with a drinking problem who was barely paying his rent in the first place. Between the two of them, I'd take him any day over the 24/7 teenager jamboree.)

After a handful of incidents, I drove over and ended the permanent party in progress, throwing out the kids and their friends. That last straw had come in the form of a complaint call that came as we were headed out on a small vacation. My kids were in the car when I stopped to lay down the law. It upset my children, watching me send more than a dozen teenagers out the door in a cloud of shouting, smoke, and profanity.

"I know my rights!" one shouted at me. "You can't do this!"

"If you don't leave," I said, "you're gonna be the one with the problem." In those days, when a Sicilian with his accent intact told you to leave – let's just say that – for once – I was grateful for the popularity of *The Godfather*.

On our return from vacation, I decided to shut it down. "I gave you a break, but it's not working," I told the woman. "Your kids are driving my tenants nuts. You have to leave." She didn't argue but said that without the apartment she had nowhere else to go. I offered to rent an inexpensive hotel room for a while but she simply had to be out of the property, not another night.

While the lady wasn't going to be a problem, I didn't know about the teenagers. I pulled in backup for my first serious "eviction." I called my landscaper, Andy, as big a guy as I knew. He would be my backup; plus, I could pay him to help me clean up the place.

We came prepared for the teenagers to call the police on us. I realized as well that in disputes like this, it is not out of the realm of possibility that the tenant stands by as the landlord gets arrested for harassment. Fortunately, none of that happened. The kids had already gone, and the show of strength wasn't necessary. Andy and I spent the next several hours filling trash bags with everything still in there, my heart sinking at the expensive and needless damage, including wrecked furniture and cigarette-burned carpet. We eventually had to gut the place. And we didn't have to pay an attorney.

I would own those apartments for another decade and a half when they would be a big part of my financial salvation in the business opportunity of my lifetime. But another major opportunity was just ahead, one that would pave the way for something even bigger.

Nice Country, America!

BECOMING AN OWNER (1982–1983)

In 1982, I reached the greatest accomplishment I had known up to that point. It remains one of the things I am proudest of having achieved. That year, I became part-owner of my first McDonald's.

This restaurant, located in Ayer, Massachusetts, was kind of a "twofer." It served the Ayer community and the population in and around nearby Fort Devens, home to about 12,000 soldiers and their families. Owning a McDonald's had been a long-time dream of mine, and now it was real. In those days, each McDonald's was a separate company. I called mine "Ayerpoli," obviously a combination of the town and my name. What a treat it was.

I couldn't have done it alone, though. Mr. McCoy and Mr. Colley had made it possible. They certainly could have owned the restaurant themselves and kept me at the level of their employee, but they took a bigger step and made me a partner. Over the years I had proven my value, and they wanted to keep me a part of their organization, and that's where I wanted to be. I had suggested that I might go out on my own, so they were aware of my interest and had asked me to be patient on the promise that when the right opportunity presented itself, they would open the door to bigger things. They were good for their word.

I've had a lot of wonderful moments in my life, but from a business perspective, my first restaurant remains among the greatest.

We always did a great job with grand openings, but I was determined to make this one a record-breaker. It was an opportunity to put my philosophy to work for a restaurant I wasn't just managing but would actually own. I would start by connecting with the community, and I got involved with anybody who would talk to me. I went to the local Chamber of Commerce to introduce myself and to see what we could do to work together for the community – it may sound hokey, but that's how I felt then and how I feel today. I reached out to the people and organizations in the Fort Devens community and the surrounding towns such as Townsend, Harvard, and Groton. We also reached out to the local newspapers who were pleased to give us lots of coverage. In one case, I was honored by a wonderful story of my life as an immigrant, coming from Sicily to eventually open my own McDonald's in the area. I wanted to reach out to all of them, but very quickly it was clear that these good people were also reaching out to me. I wanted our business to be a part of their community, and it turned out they were pleased to make our acquaintance.

One of my key supporters, a truly gracious and generous gentleman, was Lee Guercio, who owned a famous local restaurant that's still in business today. It's called The Bull Run, where the specialty is elegant family dining and superb prime rib. Lee passed away in 1990, but his restaurant still stands, and my appreciation of his kindness and guidance remains. Like me, Lee came from Sicily. That and our mutual spirit of entrepreneurism was all it took for him to befriend me and share his friendship and guidance. He really helped me in business. The night before we opened, we threw a huge cocktail party to celebrate, catered of course by Lee and his fine folks from The Bull Run. We had about 300 people – such a crowd! It was an omen of the wonderful success we would have the next morning, and in the days to come.

On opening day, we broke the regional record for sales and probably the US record as well. This was the start of a Gangbusters' run of success for the restaurant. Every evening we would send along the totals for the previous day, and every morning the McDonald's corporate office would call us, frankly in disbelief. They said that they had projected my restaurant to sell only one-third or even one-fifth of what we were reporting. They kept asking us to double check. The number of patrons seemed to outstrip what you could expect from the number of people who lived there!

I have to say though that if the corporate office was surprised, I wasn't. I was gratified that the community responded so generously to us and our outreach. This is what we had set out to do: mission accomplished.

The sales at the restaurant continued at a record-breaking pace for many years, and our success was even sweeter because of how integrated we were with the community, right from the start. We hired so many wonderful local people, and many stayed on and made a career with us. I went from being concerned with being able to make my monthly payments to starting to save money for the next opportunity. We received many accolades from the community, and people just kept coming to enjoy our delicious food and pleasant environment. It was always inspiring, motivating, and fun to visit the Ayer restaurant.

Meanwhile, the company kept growing. We were purchasing and opening new restaurants at a fast pace. In 1983, we opened or purchased four restaurants. In 1984, we opened four more. Those were exciting times – hard work but fun, for sure. We didn't think of it as a chore, the seven days a week we were out there building, opening, purchasing, and taking on new restaurants from existing owners. We just took pride in our work and appreciated the success we had found.

I should say that I skipped over the hard part, which came at the beginning when I first received the opportunity to own the Ayer restaurant. That hard part? Coming up with the money for my portion of the ownership. To cover it, I refinanced just about everything I owned. It wasn't a complicated thing to do, but it required both ingenuity and confidence, which I came to realize was the point. Mr. Colley and Mr. McCoy could have walked me through the financing, but they wanted to test me, to be sure that I had both the skill and the judgment to assume the role they were about to give me. I passed that test with flying colors.

It would not be the only financial test of my career.

* * *

There's an old saying: if all you have is a hammer, every problem looks like a nail. In other words, most of us try to solve every problem without thinking beyond the tools we have and the knowledge we possess. We don't get creative – we don't think outside the box.

If you're going to be an entrepreneur, remember this saying so you can avoid problems.

Let's say you're trying to start a business. Your accountant is going to give you their advice on the whole matter – but only from an accountant's perspective. Your lawyer is going to give you advice on the whole project, too – but only on matters related to the law. In the same way, your banker is going to weigh in on the big decision, too – from the perspective of the bank's interest.

Each professional knows a lot about his or her specialty, but it is rare that anyone is deeply knowledgeable about your business in particular. They're not as invested as you are in its success. In fact, since they are tasked to protect you from risk, they frequently provide you with reasons not to pursue the opportunity at all.

Expert advice has its place. I want to know what the banker thinks, what the lawyer thinks, and what the accountant thinks. They know things I do not. But, in the end, it is my job to collect all this advice, weigh it appropriately, and make a decision. After all, I'm the one most impacted by the decision – not just the one with the most to lose but also the most to gain.

If you consider the judgment of a one-subject expert as if they were looking at the whole situation, you're bound to make a costly mistake. A good example is how the government handled the COVID-19 pandemic. Thank goodness for the experts we had working in our government. They know things about biological research, viruses, and the scientific method that the rest of us do not know. Their knowledge no doubt saved many lives. Yet when the time came for our political leaders to decide about grave matters such as shutting down entire sections of the economy, closing schools, and consigning the elderly to living alone in their rooms for nearly two years – well, these are decisions for which science should not have been the only consideration.

We make every choice based on risk and reward. About 30,000 people die in auto accidents every year, but we don't ban automobiles, and we certainly don't ostracize people from society for taking that "risk" by driving. We have decided as a nation and a culture that, although the benefits of auto travel come with significant loss, we would rather have the benefits and some loss than no benefits and no loss. Of course, highway safety and the COVID pandemic aren't a perfect comparison, but I hope you understand what I'm trying to say. Our political leaders turned over these vital decisions to scientists with effectively no consideration for the value of human experience, education, commerce, companionship, and culture.

It's the same idea when you're making a decision for yourself about starting a business. If you leave it to the banker, the lawyer, or the accountant, you're not going to get the full picture. It is *your* job to paint that complete picture. Don't abdicate your responsibility to make a decision based on multiple inputs. As an entrepreneur, your job is to find the way to do the thing you want to do in light of everything you know about the situation – to make use of the information from various experts and stir it into a decision that must be yours and yours alone.

On top of that, it will be easier and more satisfying to take ownership of the project because, unlike the experts, your focus is not on the barriers to success but on success itself. You're thinking about how to get there, and you're motivated by the powerful desire to bring your dreams into reality. The barriers between you and your goal are not "stoppers." They are challenges to be overcome.

You have authority, opportunity, and motivation. You have knowledge and skill. And you also have your commitment to success, and that dedication will give you the extra strength you will need in the face of unanticipated adversity. If you stay on that path of commitment, nothing will stop you – nothing.

Sometimes I talk to restaurateurs who want to buy something, and they always give me the spiel about *my banker says this, my accountant says this, and my uncle or somebody says something else.* My father wasn't highly educated, but he had a lot of common sense and gave me good advice about this: tell your lawyers and your accounts only what they need to know, then take their input, not their advice. It drives me crazy when people try to put off a business decision on advisors. As the owner of a business, your decision needs to be *your* decision.

There's one more factor in making wise decisions: you need to have skin in the game. There's no motivation like having your well-being on the line.

Most restaurant franchises allow you to sign a loan through a company, and that buys you a restaurant. If at some point you can no longer pay the loan, the bank may take your restaurant, but they can't take your house.

McDonald's requires that you sign personally, with all the risk that entails. This puts the responsibility for success squarely on you. I think that's smart. If you're not confident about your capabilities, you shouldn't get into this business in the first place.

That is how, at the age of 32, I bought my first McDonald's.

MORE OPPORTUNITIES (1984-1985)

By 1984, my commitment to working hard and moving up was understood throughout the Colley/McCoy Company. I engaged in every opportunity that came my way, and I was always on the lookout for ways to advance both my career and our organization.

Now my hard work would be rewarded again, this time in the form of honor and responsibility I was excited to assume. My boss, Gary Moulton, had decided to move on. He would go out on his own and start over in Florida as a McDonald's owner-operator, far from our growing chain of restaurants in New England.

Mr. McCoy offered me the opportunity to take over Gary's role.

I would be the new vice president and director of operations, which would put me in charge of the entire Colley/McCoy Company. I would be taking over the strong team that Gary had developed and assuming what was, frankly, the best seat in the house. I would now have the best opportunity yet to learn the business. But just as important, Mr. McCoy was entrusting me, at the age of 34, with the whole of the organization he had created – at the busiest time in company history. It was like jumping onto the engine of a speeding train and taking the engineer's place without touching the brake.

But it went well. Over the next three years, we built or acquired one additional outlet for every four we already owned, placing that growth at over 25 percent.

I think it is easy to read the word "growth" and think of it as signing contracts and seeing additional revenue at the end of the month, but that's too simple. Growth is a challenging, sometimes wrenching, and always demanding process. It requires more work than anything else a business can do. When you grow, you add restaurants, and that often means starting from scratch. In this case, adding restaurants usually began with building them. To open so many new restaurants in such a short time only raises the degree of difficulty.

For each new McDonald's, we had to initiate and oversee construction, prepare for openings, establish inventories, connect with suppliers, and carry out the most challenging part, hiring an entire team including management and crew – and that list of tasks is only hitting the high spots. In most cases, we would bring in staff from other restaurants to help with training and actually to work with the new crew and management so they could learn their jobs faster. Those of us in upper management were a part of this, too, overseeing the process as well as participating in running the restaurant, and this meant that those of us involved in an opening would be at the new McDonald's seven days a week for long periods of time.

But doing this also created new opportunities for our people at every level to take on additional responsibility, both at the store level and at the supervisory level, in looking after multiple restaurants. As I say, if you wanted to move up, the opportunities were there. The senior management had done it for me when I was coming up, and I did it for those who followed me.

* * *

Part of my new position was the supervision of existing restaurants in the city of Boston. This would be the source of a difficult but valuable lesson.

Taking over supervision of the Boston restaurants would be more of a change than just turning my attention from one group of McDonald's to another. From a management perspective, these restaurants were significantly different. To this point in time, I had worked and lived in the suburbs of Leominster and Fitchburg. Those places are different in culture and style from Boston proper, and that difference extends to the challenges of running a restaurant. Customers in these different and otherwise seemingly similar places have different expectations, different attitudes, and different ways of doing things. The same goes for the employees. The city restaurants run at a faster pace, they are more intense, and the near-rural nature of the come-and-go traffic in the suburban restaurants is in strong contrast to the city restaurants, where there's less slack in the day and more frequent demands. My experience supervising and managing in the city was a bit of a shock to the system.

Part of this was driven by the times. In the early 1980s, life in the city of Boston was challenging, and that's a kind way of putting it. There were a lot of empty buildings from a slack economy, there was significant crime, and there was a fair amount of tension and unrest. Suddenly, what I had seen only on TV was right in front of my eyes. This is not to say that Boston was a frightening place – it was just a much different atmosphere than the suburbs. You had to watch yourself more carefully than you did outside the city limits.

Mr. McCoy brought me in because he thought the success I'd had in improving and maintaining our other restaurants could be applied to these restaurants, too. I remember having one of my first meetings in a Boston restaurant, the one we had on Tremont Street in a historic area across from Boston Common and the Massachusetts Statehouse. I was coming in to establish myself and offer support as the new person in charge. These people didn't know me, of course, and some of them were dubious of the "new guy." But that didn't matter. It was part of the job, to come in and set the new tone.

I gathered the management and crew and spent some time talking about new priorities. For instance, I said that we needed to do better with food quality and that we would do that by making sure we adhered to the company standards. One such standard at the time was that if a product didn't sell within a certain period of time, crew members were supposed to discard the item. I had observed some people not being as diligent as they needed to be on this – again, which is a nice way of saying that sometimes the crew would let sandwiches sit in a warmer for too long instead of discarding them and doing the work of preparing new ones. I explained what I needed them to do not by just giving them an order, though. I wanted them to understand that when you're constantly thinking in terms of the customer's experience, it makes sense to do it this way, and thus easier to remember to do it in the first place. This was hardly a difficult or unusual request. It was the kind of thing any McDonald's manager would say. Usually, employees would nod, agree, or even apologize. Not this time. My new teamed seemed to think I was bossing them around, and only because I was the "new man in charge" – and they let me know.

For a moment I was confused, but only for a moment. In Fitchburg, they knew me. We had come up through the ranks together. Here on Tremont Street, I was a stranger, just the latest boss. There was no well of goodwill I could draw from; they weren't going to assume good things about me. I had to fix this immediately, and I did. I acknowledged their concern but said that the first rule of our interactions would always be professional respect and that it would run both ways. I explained my direction once again, showing them the reflection and respect I expected them to show me. We didn't have any more problems.

Although it was awkward, it was a valuable experience for me to have, especially at the outset of my supervision of these restaurants. It was going to be a different atmosphere, and this was a good reminder. It reminded me to be confident enough to express myself, to be sure I'm being understood, and to insist on courtesy. We can all get along. We have to. But one thing wasn't going to change and could not change, not ever: I would be in charge, and they would run things the way I told them.

* * *

It's not easy for everyone to accept, but confrontation is a part of management. People respond to a mix of confident authority and humble collegiality, but not just any mix. Finding the balance requires understanding them and understanding yourself. If you seem to enjoy confrontation, you're going to get a lot more of it. But if you're afraid of confrontation, you're going to have more, too. The answer is to deal with conflict immediately by turning down the heat, asserting authority, and listening. If you can do that even before a conflict begins, you can avoid most confrontations. If you aren't being understood, don't be afraid to express yourself until it's clear to everyone.

The Boston restaurants had problems that were new to me. We saw the results of homelessness, the heartbreak of emotionally ill people living on the street, and the challenge of dealing with often-troubled people. It was hard then and, as we see more of this in the suburbs these days, it's hard now. In those days, pickpockets would jump in line and grab tourists' wallets or pocketbooks. I remember one Saturday when I was helping out behind the counter and I noticed someone in line trying to lift someone else's wallet. I caught his eye to let him know I was onto him – and he spit on me. But it wasn't to insult me, at least not entirely. He did it to create a commotion so he could finish his petty theft. Fortunately, I was able to get around the counter quickly and send him on his way. Unfortunately, these things happened more frequently than we would have liked.

I had to be a different manager from the one I'd been only days before. I had to develop thicker skin. I had to keep my eyes open. But being a good manager made a bond with the crew members there that made all these new challenges much easier.

Once I got to know the employees and they got to know me, they became truly dedicated to the work we had in common. We were connected in a positive and encouraging way. The team was a mix of teenagers and adults, and I'm proud to say that many of them stayed with us for a long, long time, and just as many would become some of the best, kindest, and most reliable employees I had known in any of my restaurants. Challenging customers became a lot less challenging with a team like that – and it had to be that way because calling the police was not a realistic option. They had more pressing things to do than come to our McDonald's, and by the time they got there the person making trouble would have been long gone.

Of course, there were times when I couldn't negotiate away somebody who wanted to get physical. I recall one afternoon in the restaurant sitting with John Lambrechts, a regional manager for McDonald's Corporation, along with John's boss. The company wanted to expand in this part of New England, and the two of them wanted my opinion about opportunities in Boston since that was the focus of my management and supervision. The conversation was going pretty well, which was good because I was a young man rising in my company who wanted to make a good impression with the higher-ups. But as we were talking, two customers across the lobby started bickering and then outright fighting.

The dispute would turn out to be urgent yet minor – but you'll see.

By this time in my Boston tenure, I was pretty confident in my ability to deal with these kinds of situations – either that or I wasn't smart enough to stay out of the middle of things. Either way, I got up from the table and, not knowing what I'd walked into, stepped between them and pulled the guys apart.

"What's the problem here?" I said to neither one in particular.

Only one answered.

"Look here," he said, wide-eyed and bouncing from foot to foot.

"Yeah?" I said.

"I have to get in there right now, and this guy won't let me!" His crisis was suddenly obvious. Fortunately, I would be able to settle it right away, and without fists. With a desperate look in his eye, he raised his finger and pointed to... the bathroom.

* * *

Almost twenty years later, I would acquire the Boston restaurants from Mr. McCoy. I held onto them until around 2011 when we too sold our holdings in that area, but I still keep in touch with many of the people I worked with there. Good people. Good times. And good lessons.

My parents wedding day
in Pietraperzia.

Joe and I playing ball in front of
our house in Pietraperzia

My grandparents, with my cousin Pietro, at their home in Pietraperzia.

Best decision of my life!

May 1971

First apartment on Third Street, Fitchburg, MA in 1963 (3rd floor).

My parents holding Melissa prior to her baptism in Leominster, MA.

My father and mother taking a chance on building a home without a building permit.

My father enjoying his garden at his home in Leominster, MA.

My son Sal, brother Joe, and Dad making wine in Leominster, MA.

Sal and Sabrina on a backpack trip in Italy during their senior year of high school.

Sal in Aruba the day he asked Sabrina to marry him.

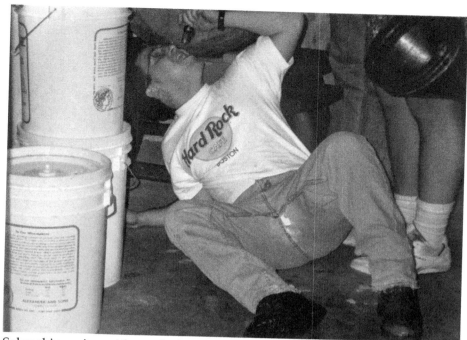

Sal making wine with my dad in Leominster, MA.

Denise and I in Sardegna at Piero and Michela's home.

At Disney World with the family.

Our first big vacation with the family - and of course, my Mother - in St. John.

Visiting my cousin Piero and friends Sardegna.

Denise and I
at my cousin
Piero's wedding
in Milan.

My parents
at my cousin
Piero's wedding
in Milan.

Tina and Jack on their wedding day at the Ritz Carlton Boston.

Sal and Sabrina's
big day!

Melissa and Dennis'
wedding at the
Boston Harbor Hotel.

Melissa and Dennis' wedding at the Boston Harbor Hotel.

Clockwise from top left:

Tina and Jack outside the church in Pietraperzia after attending my cousin's wedding.

Denise enjoying a dance with her Dad.

Our three grandchildren Peter, Sophia, and Jake at Melissa and Dennis' wedding.

Melissa, Dennis, and Colin celebrating Nolan's first communion in Concord, MA.

My mother loved being at her first great grandson Peter's birthday party.

Standing in front of my parent's tabaccheria, with apartment above, in
Pietraperzia.

Denise, my sister Rosa, and I with my Sicilian aunts, uncles, and cousin Enzo
in front of my father's land development project in Pietraperzia.

Denise, Tina, and Jack with our Italian family at their home in Milan.

Denise, Tina and I with Father Giovanni in Pietraperzia.

Denise, Tina, and Jack with my aunt and uncle in front of my grandparent's
home in Pietraperzia.

Jack and Tina join us for our trip to Sicily following their wedding.

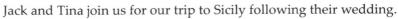

A visit to my cousin's home in Pietraperzia with a 20-course dinner.
They know how to do food!

Our 25th wedding anniversary in Hawaii with family in 1996.

Clockwise from top left:

Peter and I talking shop in Saint Lucia.

Jake and I in Orlando.

Sal and Sophia in Saint Lucia.

Lunch at Nikki Beach, St. Barth, with Sal and Sabrina, Don and Victoria, and a fun server.

Denise and I at a lunch spot at Nikki Beach in St Barth.

Celebrating our 50th wedding anniversary with family in Saint Lucia.

Our seven grandchildren – our pride and joy. Celebrating in Saint Lucia.

My granddaughter Sophia bidding up the auction at a Ronald McDonald House fundraiser.

Attending our granddaughter Chloe's grandparents' day at school.

New Hampshire
Excellence in Education
Awards

i'm lovin' it

Denise and I being recognized.

Fun times at Tina's wedding with our
banker and Santo Salamone. (below)

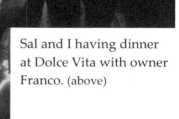

Sal and I having dinner
at Dolce Vita with owner
Franco. (above)

AMERICA AND THE IMMIGRANT EXPERIENCE (1985–1986)

My promotion to running the Colley/McCoy Company at the height of our growth made me reflect on how far I'd come and why. Then, as now, I return to the promise of the immigrant experience. I was filled with gratitude for the women and men who, having achieved the American dream, shared themselves with those who came here to pursue it, too.

Immigrants vary in education, interest, skills, and background, but almost every immigrant to America is ready to work hard. What they want, which is what I wanted when I arrived here, is to find a place where they can shine based on what they do. Not family name or where they went to school, or that they went to school at all. Not out of pity. Not because they're held to a lesser standard because of what happened to their ancestors. The world is filled with prejudice and self-centered gatekeepers, and that's a problem, but it's a problem as old as humanity. The solution, if it ever comes, will arise not from the coercion of law but from the choice we each make to be better and do better. That means not just a legal commitment but a personal, human commitment to equal treatment under the law, freedom of association, showing kindness toward one another, and the impartial sharing of access to opportunity. That's been the ideal for the pursuit of progress in America since its founding. We don't always achieve it, but we keep our eyes on that prize.

* * *

For those who believe that excellence is the first consideration, the restaurant business is a natural fit. It comes with a low barrier to entry and delivers big rewards for those willing to show up and do the job – all you have to do is decide to do it. Show me commitment and character, and I'll show you someone who's going to succeed.

It just so happens that commitment and character are the qualities that drive many people to come to America in the first place. I'm thinking especially of those immigrants who, like myself, did not or do not have the benefit of a great deal of higher education. If you're educated or bright (and often one doesn't automatically accompany the other), that's fine, too, but you don't need a credential to get into this business or find success. Many of us headed into the restaurant business because the environment made us comfortable. You can learn it as you go. A degree can impart a deeper understanding of how business works, but it's not a golden ticket. You can rise as high as you like without one. When I left college in my freshman year, it broke my parents' hearts, but I wasn't rejecting hard work or commitment, and they understood that. I was choosing my own path. I had married young, and I wanted to support my family well. I knew it would work out if I worked hard.

The restaurant business is attractive to immigrants for another reason: it minimizes the language barrier. From the beginning, our McDonald's restaurants have provided opportunities to those who can't speak English. As long as someone is good at a job and puts the customer first, we can teach them what they need to know and work around the language issue. There are things to do in a restaurant that have nothing to do with speaking English. We'd be missing an opportunity to send away a great worker on that basis.

There are other businesses like that, too. I know people who own businesses, and you do, too, that hire lots of people who don't speak English. These folks do magnificent work, often labor-intensive stuff such as roofing, painting, and landscaping. These employers provide jobs for people who need them, and sometimes the jobs become a first step toward these men and women starting businesses of their own.

* * *

I believe in America with all my heart. I display an American flag in my office. I've had one since I first had an office more than forty years ago. I have it there so everyone who comes in knows where I stand. America is the greatest country on Earth. If you come here from a country where you had no opportunity, you can start fresh in this place and make something of your life.

I'm happy that I am an American, but I'm happiest for what this means daily, what it has meant to me through the years, and what it portends for my children and their children. I have gotten to live a life of hope and opportunity made possible by this system and the men and women who came before, and this opportunity is available to anyone willing to stake a claim. I'm overjoyed with the life I've made, but I was happy forty years ago, long before I had any money in the bank, and I was happy then for the same reason I'm happy today. I take pride in the work I do, I'm happy to be busy, and I'm pleased to be making use of the opportunities I've received.

We hire foreign students in the summer for some of our seasonal restaurants, even today, and we give them all the work they want, often far beyond a normal full-time schedule. They want to make as much money as possible to take back home, and we are happy to oblige. They aren't immigrants but they are here for much the same reason: they know what's possible in America.

I wish more American parents made their children aware of just what we have compared to the rest of the world. Most people appear to take it for granted, often to the point that they don't tell their kids, let alone demonstrate to them, that we as Americans have anything special at all. The news tells you we're special, alright – special in our overwhelming faults. While we ought to try to fix our problems, the relentless focus on the bad has done damage that will take generations to unwind, if such repair is ever even attempted. Pretty soon, we'll forget the unique goodness of America; then it will have to be rediscovered and won all over again. That's the history of the fall of civilizations, though that too is something we hear little about.

I focus on the positive, though I sometimes worry that I've spoiled my children or at least my grandchildren. I may have! But whether I did or not, I'm confident that I made it clear to them just what they have as a citizen of the United States. If you're an American, too, we may very well differ on all sorts of matters of policy and politics. We may vote for different people, belong to different parties, and lend our resources and support to causes that are completely at odds. But I hope with all my heart that we share this belief: America, whatever faults she may have, is a unique place in the world and its history, that provides an opportunity – certainly imperfect at times, but an opportunity nonetheless – to anyone willing to overcome and achieve. We will always have injustice. There will never be a perfect place – but that's because there will never be perfect people.

America is the best place yet for anyone of goodwill and commitment to build a life limited only by their imagination.

Nice Country, America!

PREPARATION + OPPORTUNITY (1986–1994)

From 1986 to 1994, we held steady with about 54 restaurants, plus a few acquisitions in the last of those years. There was little growth, so you may think that I'm about to describe those years as a problem, but no. The formula is simple but undeniable: Growth = Preparation + Opportunity. You can seek growth, and you can cultivate growth, but you can't force growth. It comes only out of its two components.

During the late 80s and 90s, opportunities for acquisitions came less frequently, attractive offers even less so. But that was not necessarily a bad thing. You can't expect to go like gangbusters every year. It just doesn't happen that way.

So we looked deeper into what was happening and discovered an opportunity.

We continued preparing for growth, adjusting the company to be ready for whatever might come our way. We also invested resources in providing extra support, education, and training for our management and executive folks, and filling out their ranks. We kept our heads down and kept the business well in the black.

That said, there was one purchase in those years I have to mention, one bit of key growth. It would be the key to the next big advancement in my life.

In 1993, we opened a restaurant near Ayer, Massachusetts, in Townsend. Mr. McCoy gave me the opportunity to partner on that restaurant as well, in part because of the location: as you may remember, I already owned the Ayer restaurant. It was where I had started "Ayerpoli." Now I would own another restaurant nearby.

I wasn't exactly a business kingpin, but owning a pair of McDonald's is a significant accomplishment... That they were located where I began my McDonald's career only made the success sweeter.

With this acquisition, preparation, and opportunity were about to meet again in a wonderful way.

* * *

To become a McDonald's owner-operator, you have to go through the process of being approved. That means demonstrating by doing – operating and managing every aspect of a "live" McDonald's restaurant – for a panel at corporate headquarters. This of course is the famous "Hamburger University." They first certify you as an owner-operator for one restaurant, then you have to show that you're capable of running an entire organization.

With my business now including ownership of two restaurants, I needed to make some plans. Ownership of the restaurants wasn't simply an asset someone could inherit. It came with requirements imposed by the simple fact that a busy, high-profile restaurant in a global brand has to be run closely and carefully by someone who knows what they're doing. That is the purpose of Hamburger U.

A little before this time, my son, Sal, had graduated from Northeastern University in Boston. It was clear where his interests lay. He had studied entrepreneurism. Since then, he had succeeded in other positions, including a fantastic turn in a co-op program, showing me he had gained the maturity and self-discipline you hope for in your children.

But when it comes to selecting a business partner, you can't just hope. You have to be sure.

I'm proud to tell you that I had already seen those qualities in Sal. I remember where the seeds were planted, on weekends doing basic chores, such as cleaning out the garage. No matter what Sal had been up to the night before in his high school years, I'd have him out there with me the next day, giving him a lesson by doing so. I wanted him to understand the truth: our enthusiasm for a job may rise and fall, but responsibilities remain and we have to meet them.

I doubt I ever said those words to him. I believe that words aren't nearly as important as actions. What you want people to do, you show them. What they see you doing, head down, mouth shut – that's the commitment that makes an impression. Sal had seen me commit myself to professional success – not talking about it but doing it. His mother and I – and his grandfather, too – had lived the example he saw each day. Sal had now expressed an interest in joining the business. I'm happy to tell you that it was clear that he was ready.

The truth is I needed him to be. It was important to me that Sal be qualified to take over if, God forbid, something were to happen.

We employ a lot of people, and our restaurants are responsible for a great deal of economic activity: there are families who depend on the jobs our restaurants provide. We needed to protect that.

I wanted Sal to go through the qualification process at the corporate level, Hamburger University, but I didn't send him there immediately. Though many owners who have multiple restaurants make that move pretty quickly, I held off.

I didn't want to send him to headquarters to learn. I wanted to send him there to show what he could already do.

I wanted Sal to be a master not just at running a McDonald's restaurant but also at operating a group of McDonald's. When I felt comfortable that he could own and operate a group of McDonald's and I had seen that he was qualified to take over if circumstances required him to step into the lead role, I finally had him apply.

This next part may surprise you. When I finally sent Sal to go through that certification, he understood that he was not coming back to the office to assume a partnership. This was a preparation, not a coronation. That made for an interesting question and a telling response. While he was at the training, someone with the corporate operation asked him why he was going through this demanding program even though he didn't own any pieces of his family operation back home.

His answer tells you all you need to know about his readiness for the job I had in mind for my oldest son.

"Good things come to those who are prepared," said my son. It was the right answer. I could not have been prouder.

* * *

Sal will tell you that ever since he was young, he dreamed that he might join me and then, someday, make it possible for the two of us to go out on our own. To tell you the truth, that had become my dream, too. But we would have to bide our time for a while, in part to get used to the possibility of this huge dream becoming reality. We would also have to apply the tried-and-true formula: practicing preparation while waiting for and cultivating the right opportunity.

The years in between would prove to be an exciting journey, but heartache was coming soon.

REMEMBERING MY WONDERFUL FATHER
(1994)

In February of 1994, I lost my dad. It was a surprise for all of us.

He was 78 and generally healthy, though there had been signs of trouble. In the months before, he'd had more frequent difficulties not unusual for a man his age. On occasion, he might say he wasn't feeling well. A few times this led to an immediate examination and some of those led to a short hospital visit. That said, each concluded with doctors telling us they didn't know what the problem might be. Then they would discharge him, and we'd take him home. When we got there, he'd say that he felt fine – and I believe he did.

The night before the morning of his passing, my mother called me for some help. Given her concern for Dad, this wasn't unusual. She would ring up my sister or me – not so often my younger brother, as he lived far away – and ask one of us to stay over in case Dad had trouble. She didn't feel comfortable dealing with it alone. This night, she called me. After a late night at work, I came right over. I said hello to my mother, then checked in on Dad. I was pleased to find him in great spirits. He wanted to chit-chat about things, which always pleased both of us, but at the end of a long day, I was tired. "It's nine o'clock, Dad," I said. "Let's get some sleep and we'll talk tomorrow night. I'll come home early and we'll have dinner. It'll be good." He was fine with that. Sicilians like family, food, and conversation. My father and I were no exceptions.

The next morning, I headed home before going to work. While between my parents' place and my own, the cell phone rang. Denise was calling on behalf of my mother. Mom wasn't good with the phone and in this stressful moment, she let my wife help her. "Your dad's not feeling well," Denise said. "Your mom wants you to go back home."

"Oh, is that it?" I said. "I thought you were checking up on me because I didn't come home last night!" We liked to tease each other and still do, but something about this moment was different. The mood didn't feel as light.

"Your mother needs you over there," she said. I turned the car around.

By the time I arrived, Dad had already passed. The cause was a heart attack. We called an ambulance anyway. It's what you do. They came quickly. We were grateful for that. They made every attempt to resuscitate him but without success.

My father lived a long, productive life. He set all of us kids on a path to meaning, satisfaction, and happiness. He taught us right from wrong. We learned how to conduct ourselves in life not just from his words but also, most importantly, from his deeds. He set an example by the way he lived. My father's example defines what, to me, is a life well lived.

* * *

My dad came to America to create success for himself. Though I think he was happy with the success he found, it definitely wasn't the success he had in mind. He made one of those trades that heads of families sometimes make: they want something for themselves, but they sacrifice some of that to first honor their obligations. For most people, at least the ones I respect, when that obligation comes into conflict with their other goals, they do the right thing.

My dad didn't find all of what he was looking for, but he loved the things he found instead. I believe that this gave him meaning and satisfaction and joy.

By bringing his family to America, Dad was making a gamble. He and my mother gave up a comfortable life. Back in Sicily, my dad was somebody, so coming here as just another fellow fresh off the boat was especially difficult. Dad came here in his mid-40s, an age when it is difficult to learn a new language. All his friends were Italian. At home, we spoke Italian. He had a lot to learn.

Then there was the matter of pride. My dad, a busy entrepreneur in Sicily, was now a factory worker in a place he did not know. I'm not saying he was some big captain of the industry over there, but in our small town, he had achieved significant success. He stepped back from that and had to adjust. Yet he was independent in his work and his spirit, and that carried him through this difficult beginning.

My father didn't become the great entrepreneur he hoped to be, but he did something more: he established roots for his family and made it possible for his children, grandchildren, and all who would come after to pursue their dreams unfettered. By any definition, my father was a success. So, yes, his trip to America was a gamble, but there was a lot of selflessness in it as well.

There's something to be proud of, being a man like that, and I will always be grateful for what he gave us.

* * *

Here's one more story about Dad. It's about one of his entrepreneurial efforts that paid off handsomely.

My dad was involved in real estate. (If you noticed that over the years the Napolis occasionally dabbled in real estate, now you know how it started.) Just before we left Sicily, he had identified a piece of property outside of town he thought was desirable. He figured he could buy it, develop it, then sell it for a profit, thus bankrolling us in our new home.

He went looking for people who, like him, might want to invest in something worthwhile of their own. He'd find a potential buyer and he'd say, "One of these days, people are going to come around wanting a country home. If you buy up this land, you can subdivide it into lots for that and sell them at a nice profit." But nobody bought his pitch so, after a while, he bought the land himself, figuring that if nobody else wanted to take advantage of the opportunity, he would. "I think this can happen," he said. He kept that investment in his back pocket, so to speak, and we left for America.

After we had been here for a while, having learned a few hard lessons but now on track in our new home, he went back to Italy and developed that land. He had it carved into house lots, and he made money.

But it wasn't as simple as finding a buyer. There would be a problem to overcome.

He had the land professionally subdivided, but the people who ran the town wouldn't give him the official permissions he needed to put houses there. He decided to call their bluff. He said, "I'm going to build a house. We'll see if they make me tear it down just because it's not an approved subdivision." So that's what he did, and to make it even harder for them to make him raze the property, he raised the stakes. He sold several of the house lots to relatives at a low price so they too could build houses. This way, the town fathers would have to tell a whole group of people to tear down brand-new houses. Dad was betting they wouldn't have the stomach to do it. And Dad was correct. Dad worked hard, but he also worked very, very smartly.

My dad was a risk-taker, but a clever one.

And a very successful one, too.

* * *

I tell my kids that they have no bad examples from my family.

There's my older brother, who went to the university and became a successful plastics engineer.

Or consider my sister, who went to beauty school. Then, instead of going to work for someone else, she got her beauty operator's license and opened her own shop – and did so while working in a clothing factory to pay the bills. She worked independently as a beauty operator for her entire career.

Or look at the success of my younger brother. When he graduated from high school, he obtained a real estate license and worked first from our parents' sun porch – really! He then opened up his own business, a choice that, by that time, had become almost a family tradition. He grew his operation to about 10 real estate offices until he changed course about 20 years ago to become a McDonald's owner-operator. At the time of this writing, he owns 18 stores, and by the time you read this, he probably owns even more.

As for me, well – you know my story. These days, my son and I, along with my family, are McDonald's owner-operators with 67 stores.

* * *

My dad remains in our hearts and lives through the traditions we all created and sustain as a family.

One of the things I've told my children and grandchildren is that it matters what you do with your loved ones while they're still with you. My sorrow at Dad's passing was deep and profound. As I share this with you, I feel that sadness rising once more. You don't move past such a loss. You learn to live with it, to make room for it in your heart so it doesn't hurt so much. But one of the ways you find peace is that you retreat in memory to the wonderful days you shared.

Create good times with the ones you love. Make memories. Take joy in every moment. Share your heart, and hold fast to theirs.

Vacations, fancy dinners, day trips – those are obvious. But you'll be surprised what you'll ultimately recall as the best times. Remember that language barrier? Who would have thought that a problem like that would turn out to be the source of so many happy memories in so many places? My folks' need for a translator led to moments we ended up helping, smiling, laughing, and bonding – whether in a law office, a business transaction, a doctor's office, or just a store. All that connected us even more.

Of course, many memories and traditions are entirely intentional. Denise and I named our son, Sal, after my father. If you run into Sal, ask him to show you his money clip. On it, you will find a picture of his namesake, my dad.

When Sal and his wife Sabrina were about to have their first son in 2003, I teased them that they had to follow the family tradition and name the child after me. Sal, who gives as good as he gets, teased me right back: "I may have only one son, Dad. I think maybe I should name him after myself!"

My father, as if on cue in a comedy sketch, said, "I don't blame the boy!"

Boy, did I blow my stack! *What about tradition? What about our Italian heritage? You can't do that, son!* By the time I cooled down, I realized they had had quite a laugh at my expense, and of course, I thought it was funny, too – but not at first. Which made it even funnier for them.

In case I haven't mentioned it, I'm proud to tell you that Sal and Sabrina did in fact name their firstborn son after me, and Peter makes me proud.

* * *

We respect and love family tradition, from the way we name our children to the trips and get-togethers that we anticipate throughout the year. It's important to enjoy time together. We take winter trips every year, and we spend a portion of each summer at our home on the Cape. Then there's Christmas. Denise and I love Christmas morning. What grandparent doesn't? Everyone comes over to the house, and I take over the kitchen to cook.

But our traditions aren't all major events. They don't have to be. To me, dinner at home is a celebration. Having family over is a celebration. Any time with my loved ones is time well spent.

Those moments bring me joy, and they take me back to times with my dad.

* * *

My father was a pillar of strength for me and all of us. He was a man of wise judgment. He made my life better – he made my life possible. But getting through my sorrow was easier because I had so many good times to recall. He lived life to the fullest. His beautiful, loving, and ever-growing family will continue to live life to the fullest. This is the tradition that matters most, and it came from my father. He taught me that living life in this way is the wisest investment I will ever make.

Rest well, Dad. Rest well.

BECOMING A PARTNER (1994)

My father's passing made 1994 a difficult year. Only ten months later, my brother-in-law, John, fell to cancer, a good man taken too soon.

There's a lesson in every loss, and I found one in John's passing so soon after my father: get busy. None of us knows how long we have here, so follow your dreams. Don't wait for the perfect moment because it will never be perfect enough. Start now. In some cases, opportunity will be thrust upon you, so it's wise to always be preparing.

1994 would bring one of those moments, the payoff of years of work and preparation. The sweet would arrive in the midst of the bitter. It would be up to me to navigate the challenge. In that year, I spent a lot of time asking myself what my father would do, how he would conduct himself, and what he would choose in various situations. I was pleased to find that there wasn't much thinking to do about that. After a lifetime of living his advice, the right answers came naturally.

Dad was my greatest mentor and most influential example. He gave me the gift of common sense. Don't overcomplicate things. Don't talk yourself out of a good opportunity. He also showed me how to figure out when and how to take risks, when brains matter more than intuition, and when it's intuition all the way –

call it relying on blood and guts. I would have to be tough, and again his example showed me the way because when things got tough, my father got tougher. I would think often of how his life in America began. He had been making a comfortable living in Sicily when he packed up in his mid-40s for America, brought along a family of six to provide for, and pursued his dream. What a combination that took! Courage, fortitude, and judgment.

Most of all, it took blood and guts.

I was going to need that.

* * *

The bloom of my professional life in 1994 began with a seed planted the year before. At the end of 1993, Mr. McCoy informed me that he and Mr. Colley were going to end the partnership that had begun nearly three decades earlier in 1967. This was traumatic news. I had "grown-up" professionally under the Colley/McCoy brand. But while we had enjoyed a wonderful history together, I knew to be open to new opportunities.

Life is filled with moving on and moving up, and this corporate shift was key to that for these two men and their families. Mr. McCoy had a son in the business. Mr. Colley had three. The restructuring was best for their families. I wished them well. But there was something in it for me, too. The end of the partnership would be the beginning of another. That would create a life-changing opportunity for me.

As usual with such things, it came with a challenge.

* * *

The terms of the restructuring were simple. Mr. Colley would keep the 13 New York restaurants the joint company had held. Mr. McCoy and I would take the 53 New England restaurants. This would come about through a buyout financed by Mr. McCoy and myself. With that came the challenge: I was going to have to find the cash to join the new company as a partner. The new venture would be worth $60 million. As a junior partner, I would hold 5 percent of the operation.

That meant I would need to come up with cash and assets worth $3 million.

But before I tell you how I was able to take advantage of this offer, let me tell you why it came to me in the first place.

Let's be clear, Mr. McCoy could have made another choice. For instance, he could have purchased the whole operation himself. After all, this wasn't a gamble on an unproven new business. This was a restructuring under a historic, international brand that wasn't going anywhere but up. By taking on minimal risk and only a little additional responsibility, he could have retained all the benefits. Or he could have given the opportunity I got to someone else, as long as the partner was committed to working hard to build on what had been achieved so far.

But there was another consideration in play. Mr. McCoy was preserving and expanding the organization and influence he and Mr. Colley had built. This was a company that had become a part of dozens of communities, and that had made possible many opportunities, from a first job to an entire career, for thousands of individuals and families throughout the northeastern United States, our home. I think that's why he didn't just keep it all for himself. Why me? The way to ensure the continuation of those "bigger things" – not just the financial things but the things built on what he believed in – was to take the first step in a generational handoff to someone of like mind and character.

Looking at it that way, all we had done over the years had been leading to this moment, naturally. It made sense to find a partner who could carry on, and that person would be someone who had already contributed significantly to the company's success, shared Mr. McCoy's passion, commitment, and principles, and had earned the opportunity.

In this way, our relationship was both personal and professional. It wasn't that we went to lunch every day or played cards on the weekend – it wasn't like that. It was about important things such as commitment to community, a shared set of priorities about how to do business, a sense of obligation to those around us, a belief in doing the right thing regardless, and a love of our country – those deeper things that affect how a man or a woman conducts his or her life each day. Yes, I was effective at what I did. He was comfortable having me as his right-hand man to help run the organization and the restaurants. And we had a good connection. So perhaps the best way to think about it is that the match made sense because, in so many things, he was comfortable with me, and I was comfortable with him. I had been working for the company since 1969. There's a reason for that kind of longevity: the connection just worked.

As for Mr. Colley, I have to admit I didn't know him as well, but there was a good reason for that: geography. Mr. McCoy and Mr. Colley had an efficient, simple setup: McCoy ran things in New England, where I was, and Colley ran things in New York. They created efficiencies (and additional profit) by sharing responsibilities and expenses so they could do better together. I would see Mr. Colley at Christmas parties and store openings – always impressive, and indispensable to the company's success.

I met Mr. McCoy when he bought the Fitchburg restaurant where I was a teenage member of the crew behind the counter. He had dropped by around ten or maybe eleven at night, checking in on his restaurant after spending an evening at a public hearing to get clearance for some construction. Even as a young man, I was impressed with someone working with that kind of commitment – and that late at night! – and doing it with a smile on his face. Here was the man at the top of the organization down here in the trenches with the rest of us. Believe me, that made an impression that would last a lifetime.

Not long after that, Mr. McCoy opened the Leominster restaurant. It seems I had made enough of an impression on him, even at a distance, that he sent me there as a member of management – and I was still in high school. He recognized something of value, and I was making a difference in my job. He was impressed with me, it seems. I was certainly impressed with him. A few years later, he came into where I was working, and I told him that I needed to leave because I was taking my wife out to dinner for our first wedding anniversary.

"Where are you taking her?" he said. I mentioned a restaurant in the next town over, a place that would take more than a few minutes to reach. He sent me on my way, and I drove to the house to pick up Denise. But when we arrived at the restaurant, we got a surprise. When we stopped by the bar for a pre-dinner cocktail, there was Mr. McCoy. He greeted us and wished us a happy anniversary, then told us that our anniversary dinner would be on him.

Early on, he and I had a special bond and mutual respect. Obviously, it made such a difference in my life. Because of that, I've made it a priority in my own life to make such connections with the young people who work for me, the way I worked for him. I look for the ones who make it clear that they're willing to work hard for success – the ones who have what it takes.

* * *

I needed $3 million. To make my end of the deal, it would take all the business acumen and goodwill I'd accumulated in a lifetime – and all the money, too.

To me, this next step was a small step built on confidence, but from the outside, it may have looked like a leap of faith. It began with having to sell everything I owned. I'm not talking about putting our couch in a yard sale or pawning Denise's wedding ring. I mean the profit-generating assets I'd accumulated to earn a living as I built my career.

I owned two McDonald's restaurants. Selling them would get me a lot of what I needed, so I put them in. In addition, I owned a small summer house. It was nothing big or flashy but it had value, so I sold it as well. Next up was the home we lived in. It was already heavily mortgaged, but there was a bit more we could borrow against, so I did that, too. My father had invested in real estate, so I had, too. By 1994, I had held as many as 18 apartments in several buildings, some purchased many years before. The properties had appreciated, and I was earning monthly income from their rent. Those had to go, too.

Everything including change in the couch cushions: that's what I put on the table to buy into my end of the deal. But even that wasn't enough. When all the cashing-in was completed, I still did not have the money I needed for the share Mr. McCoy had made available. I would have to find another quarter-million dollars – or settle for a much smaller piece of the company that I had helped bring this far, one that I wanted to build upon even more. All that meant I would need a big loan – but without collateral, getting a loan is impossible.

Well, almost impossible.

My first stop was at my regular bank, a good-sized operation that could afford both the loan and the associated low-risk. But that was just my opinion. The final decision would come down to the banker. In situations like this, when there's no collateral, it's a judgment call that depends on subjective opinions about business history, the character of the borrower, and the appetite for a risk-versus-reward opportunity, which rests more on insight than the numbers on the page. When we sat down, I was direct: I was asking for the loan – not based on optimism and crossed fingers over some idea. I wasn't even asking based on some brand-new business plan. I was asking them to enable me to acquire a portion of a thriving operation that I had helped build, one already backed by the most famous brand in the world, a true global enterprise. I was thinking big picture, but as usual, Mr. McCoy knew that sometimes the small things matter as much. "Pete's good for it," he said, which has meaning only when it comes from someone like him, someone who would be as invested in all this as the bank. If that weren't enough, Mr. McCoy had also taken on McDonald's Corporation as a silent partner, not just enhancing but fairly gilding the security of this new organization.

But that wasn't enough for this banker, or for the bank that had stood by us until this point. They couldn't find the appetite. Without collateral, he said, this was a non-starter. And that was that. If strike one was coming up short in the first place on my own assets, strike two was getting turned down by our best-bet bank, the place we'd been using for years.

Our last chance – rather, my last chance – would come from a most unlikely source. It was a small, community bank, a local operation based in Ayer.

When I bought my first McDonald's in Ayer, Massachusetts, a dozen miles to the east of where I started in Leominster and Fitchburg, I got deeply involved with the community. For future purchases, this became second nature. When I open or acquire a McDonald's in any location, one of the first things I do is get involved with the community, connect with the people who live there, and make my restaurant a part of their lives. You may not drive past McDonald's and think, "Boy, I sure hope they're involved in my community," but the thing is that the people who work at any McDonald's and who eat at the restaurant are a part of the community, and it's easier to be a part of the commerce in a community if you make common cause with the people who live there.

It's not very smart to just show up somewhere and start selling things. We ought to be a part of the community we're joining. We're not hawking trinkets out of the trunk of a car wherever we can find a place to park. Our restaurants are integrated into people's lives. When you think of your daily routine, McDonald's may come to mind, whether it's grabbing coffee on the way to work, settling in for a fast and tasty lunch at a fair price, taking the kids' ball team for a bite after the Saturday game, or pretty much anything else. The neighborhood McDonald's restaurant is integral to the life of a community. We ought to build up that connection. My Ayer restaurant was my first McDonald's. My experience there set the standard for how I would do business for the rest of my life, starting with being a part of the community. This would be the moment when those community roots went from being not only the right thing to have done. These roots proved to have been a wise investment in my future.

I went to the bankers I knew from buying the Ayer McDonald's. The senior loan officer and the president of the bank took me in right away. I explained the situation: mortgaged to the hilt with nothing left to borrow against and a balance due right away. The alternative for me was to lose the opportunity I had been working toward my whole life.

"You know how I do business," I said. "And you know me. You know I'm a part of this community and that I'm not going anywhere. Based on the example you've seen, you know that if you loan me what I need, I'll pay you back."

Business isn't just what the experts say, and decisions are not just a matter of filling in the boxes and seeing what the spreadsheet spits out. The best decisions are made by factoring in everything you know. That's what I did, and that's what those bankers did.

The president and senior vice president in charge of commercial loans for this small-town bank, Middlesex Savings, came through for me. They gave me an "unsecured" loan, meaning it was granted based on the credit and character of the person applying. The big bank that I had first approached had refused. But this bank, rooted in a community where I belonged, took a chance on me because it wasn't a chance at all. It was a judgment based on experience. I walked out with a check for $250,000.

I was now a partner – a relatively small partner, but an owner nonetheless. I held a stake in all 53 New England McDonald's restaurants. I've had a lot of great moments in my career and my life, and this one may be the best of all.

* * *

I remember talking to Mr. McCoy when he had first told me about the reorganization, or as I called it, the split. He didn't like that term, not at all.

He and I used to get together on Saturdays in the office to work and catch up. I told him that I thought it was crazy to give up this wonderful company. He told me that "giving it up" was the wrong way to think about it. He was changing things because circumstances had changed.

"It'll be good, Pete," he said. "Good for my family, good for the Colleys, good for business. And it will be very good for you."

As usual, he was right. This new enterprise meant a new role for me in the organization. As they say, I got kicked upstairs. Mr. McCoy would be the operations partner, making all the business decisions. As the minority partner, I would be in charge of the restaurants. I took the title of vice president and director of operations. My responsibilities matched well with my experience and interest. I made sure that our 53 restaurants were operating the way they should, that the facilities were in good repair, that our employees were meeting our standards and pursuing our priorities, and that we were meeting their needs so they could do their job.

A big part of this was ensuring that all staff, management, crew, and supervisors were well-trained and motivated. We met often and at every level. I did not hesitate to consider, or reconsider, the requirements for any job in the restaurants. I had done them all. I like encouraging and incentivizing people to do a good job – I liked doing it then, and I like doing it now. In my new role, I spent a lot of time doing that, not only with the folks in the restaurants but also with the supervisors. The latter was especially important because their job was to make sure our corporate goals and outlook were carried out at the restaurant level. Thus, I spent time explaining not only what our priorities were but also how to improve the customer experience by acting on them. That meant spending time on practical ways to improve productivity, food safety, customer satisfaction, excellence in performance, and training and development of our people.

Which is to say that all this kept me busier than I'd ever been, and this, in turn, had an unexpected upside: I had no time to dwell on the sadness I felt after my dad and my brother-in-law had passed. When could I have done so, anyway? I had so little time for anything but work that when I thought of Dad and John, I focused on the good times. Thank God for tiny-but-mighty favors.

I had achieved one of my biggest dreams. It had come out of the ashes of a tragic year, but somehow, I was busier – and more satisfied – than ever before. Life will always come with sadness. What matters is making life count. In doing that, we honor those who've gone, those we love. In that way, they will always be with us.

FOR BETTER, FOR WORSE (1995-2001)

After the previous twelve months, I was happy to see 1995 arrive. It would be the biggest growth year so far in the history of the company.

Soon after we reorganized and I became a partner, we opened several new restaurants but with a twist: many were small-location sites, what we call "satellites." This included one inside a Walmart, a couple in strip malls, and one in Salisbury Beach, Mass. That one was a tiny operation, more like the hamburger stand of three decades before. (It was also the location that introduced us to Jeremy Hinton, who worked there as a manager and has since risen to become our president). We were taking calculated risks, vital to sustaining a business.

So, in addition to looking after our 53 restaurants, I was also overseeing the construction and acquisition of 14 new outlets – ordering equipment, hiring new employees, setting up training, and identifying experienced folks in our other restaurants to work with the new people. As always, I worked to encourage everyone to work toward our constant goal of pleasing our customers.

It was tough, but we got it done, in large part because the McDonald's system is so, well, *good*. It runs like a well-oiled machine. Then as now, that system makes it easy for us to build, train, organize, and open because it is a systematic process that takes on every issue that needs attention. Because of that McDonald's system, we're not reinventing the wheel every time we expand to a new location.

We finished 1995, a year of record expansion, with 67 units. 1996 and 1997 were almost as busy. We opened 5 new restaurants each of those years but we had to close some of the satellites. Most had produced disappointing returns, especially considering the cost of moving experienced people to them from other locations and the high volume of staff in light of low revenues.

I wouldn't say that the experiment did not work. I'd say that we learned better what works and what doesn't. That's a valuable thing, and failure is the wrong word for something that generates value.

* * *

Thirty-seven years after we came to America, the world arrived at the end of the 20th century. We're more than two decades past it now, and it still feels strange to say! Yet the last decades of the 1900s seem no further in the past than yesterday.

I feel as hopeful today as I did twenty years ago, as hopeful as I did as a young owner-operator, as hopeful as I did as a teenager who was grateful for that first crew job that helped me contribute to the family income and put some gas in the car for a Friday night. And this wonderful business is still growing, still flexible, and still focused on the future.

As the 20th century ended, we remained full speed ahead on our strategy for growth and success, acquiring promising restaurants when the opportunity was ripe and trimming underperforming locations to keep things lean. In 1996, we acquired 5 restaurants and parted with 1, bringing us to 71 outlets. The next year, we acquired 5 more and cut 2, which raised the count to 74. Over the next 24 months, we acquired 6 and cut 6, and that is where things would remain for the next few years, hovering just above 70 locations in the years after the turn of the century.

Of course, change remained a constant. It was around this time that corporate headquarters announced an aggressive move to keep the brand relevant in the new century. It would require financial sacrifice from the owner-operators. For those of us who owned many restaurants, the demand was not just eye-popping but also nearly budget-busting: McDonald's would require vast numbers of restaurants to be razed and rebuilt.

Not just updated: rebuilt.

At first, we weren't too concerned. We thought it would apply only to the older units; older than, say, Fitchburg, which you may recall was Unit #466 out of about 30,000 around the world. We soon learned that this was a judgment we needed to make in partnership with McDonald's based on the condition of the physical plant. The cost for each restaurant would be about $2 million, which is about $3.4 million today. I'll leave the math to you.

We did the work. We didn't have a choice. It was scary. But in hindsight, it was a wise move. The expense was considerable, but the ledger eventually showed the value of the upgrade. It's an excellent example of the importance of focusing on the goal, not the problem. McDonald's founder Ray Kroc always demanded we keep things "green and growing." He was right once again.

That modernization campaign was the first of several over the years. Subsequent efforts have more often been to add features than to raze a building and start again. I think of that "21st century rebuild" as a foundation for what has come since: modernization to meet the sophisticated and changing demands of our customers. Sometimes it's a modification to the drive-thru, such as adding two lanes or enhancing the look and feel of our dining rooms. Sometimes it's for adding or accommodating technology, such as installing kiosks in the dining room or dedicating parking slots for customers who order on our McDonald's app and want food delivered to their car. Occasionally, we make changes to how we do things, and those don't usually require construction. For instance, in recent years, we've added table service. And, yes, there are still occasional big overhauls of the way things look, inside and out.

Typically, change is good. When it's not, my job is to find the good and create value from whatever we're facing – to focus on the solution, not the problem. Does change lead to something better every time? No, but that's okay. Growth doesn't happen in a straight line. The successful moments come with not-so-successful moments.

For better, for worse.

* * *

Yet this new century also began with horror.

If you were born in the 20th century, you remember where you were at the first tragic event of the 21st century. On September 11, 2001, the world changed forever with the horrific attack on our country by terrorists – men of pure evil – crashing fully loaded passenger jets into the World Trade Center Towers I and II in New York and the Pentagon in Washington DC. There was a fourth crash as well, one that cost lives but prevented even more loss of life when brave passengers sacrificed themselves by taking control from the terrorists and forcing down their aircraft in a field near Shanksville, Pennsylvania.

I was driving alone that morning, on my way to an advertising meeting at our local McDonald's corporate office in Westwood, Mass. Sal called my cell phone – still something I was new to carrying around – to tell me the news.

"That's impossible," I said. "This must have been an accident."

"Dad," he said, "I don't think it is. I'm watching on TV."

He was right, but it was hard for me to accept. You might as well have told me that the sun didn't rise. That's how I feel about our country: some things are just not possible.

But suddenly the impossible had happened, and on a sunny morning only a few hundred miles from where I sat. Many of us had our thinking changed that day. What we thought about our way of life, and the security of this life, was transformed. Growing up in Sicily, you hear a lot of different things about violence, gangs, and such, even in a small town like ours. Wherever you go there are sometimes accidents and sometimes murders, but not often is there anything like this. I certainly didn't imagine it happening in my adopted country. The sad, anger-making news was almost too difficult to bear. Our President, George W. Bush, did a wonderful job of uniting the country and making us feel more confident to return to our daily routines.

Like everyone else, we moved ahead, though now we were a little more careful, a little more wary, and a little less confident in our idealism. The world had changed, and for once, sadly, it wasn't just something people say after a tragedy. This was the biggest one any of us had seen. Things would be different.

* * *

The day-to-day rhythm of running a business was now overshadowed by the possibility of terrorism. This took the form of bringing a little more suspicion to uncertain situations, usually by keeping in mind that it was better to be safe than sorry when coming across unknown packages, unusual situations, or, and I'm being candid here, people acting in some strange or perhaps unbalanced way. Things that previously had been of no concern were now red flags – potential signs of an impending act of terror. Call it "practical paranoia." Or self-protection.

Later in 2001, we were fortunate to encounter a promising opportunity: a major project on the Massachusetts Turnpike. We would take over food concessions for a location there and build a brand new, state-of-the-art McDonald's restaurant to accommodate travelers. Any other time I would have considered this all gain and no pain, but times had changed. I would be putting employees on a busy highway where thousands of people and vehicles would be able to pull in anytime, unannounced and, most troubling, unexamined.

But here's the thing. After 9/11, each person had to decide whether to live in confidence or fear. There was a popular phrase around that time that quickly became cliché: if we avoid doing *thus and so*, the terrorists win. It was a way to remind ourselves that life had to go on. Sure, there were new risks, but after a time we realized that the risks were also remote. If we started making our lives smaller and smaller, the terrorists truly would have achieved their goals. After all, the goal is in the name. They weren't just here to kill people but to inflict physical and mental terror. So we had to grow accustomed to living life, not limiting life, in this new environment.

Being near that highway was scary, and, yes, it came with additional risks. But we did it anyway. My mission for our restaurants has always been to serve people. It's not always about selling food and the pursuit of the bottom line.

As I always say, some things you do because they're the right things to do.

If we were to carry on and do the right thing here, providing a restful place for people to grab a meal or a snack, sit and rest for a moment, or just take advantage of a clean restroom along their journey, we'd be doing what we do best. So that's what we did.

Those years were years of change – good years, sometimes for better and sometimes for worse – but always toward better things. Those better things are often just ahead and nearly always come with a challenge.

THE BIRTH OF THE NAPOLI GROUP
(2002-2003)

On a Saturday morning in late 2002, Mr. McCoy came into my office as he had so many Saturdays before. But this conversation would be different.

"Peter," he said, "are you ready to take over?"

It was a question I had anticipated for years, and with a mixture of excitement and sadness. This question came with great promise, opportunity, and responsibility. He was asking me to continue the joint venture we shared with McDonald's, but now on my own. In addition, he was asking me to buy out the New England outlets and assume ownership of all 73 restaurants. Those were the exciting and challenging parts. The sad part? The most significant, rewarding, and wonderful professional relationship of my life would be coming to an end.

It was a life-changing question that deserved a lot of thought, but that wouldn't delay my answer. He and I already knew what I would say. He and I had spent a lifetime preparing for this moment.

I thought back on the more than three decades we had spent working together – from my earliest days as a teenager in the 1960s working as a crew member to his decision to move me into management. I thought of how he then added to my responsibilities, testing my abilities until he moved me into higher and higher leadership roles – and now, here he was, offering me the reigns to run everything.

How had he built such an organization? He had been committed to his customers, employees, community, and doing the right thing. He had worked hard. I thought of an evening in 1970 when I was a manager at the Leominster restaurant. It was well past midnight, but there was Mr. McCoy, still working – even after almost all of the crew had gone home.

I thought of that night in 1972 when I wanted to leave early to take my wife to our anniversary dinner and how Mr. McCoy not only sent me on my way but also showed up at the restaurant to buy us dinner and wish us well. Over the years, Mr. McCoy had gone from being my boss to my friend, and now we were colleagues and men of like minds in so many things. His offer was, therefore, not only an opportunity – it was an endorsement and gratitude for the work we'd done together for a lifetime.

Was I ready to take over? I thought so, and he did, too. That reduced the question to one whose answer I knew for certain. Would I step up and take over? My answer: an absolute and confident *yes*.

There was one more thing, though – one more opportunity that I wanted to create, but not for me.

In 1994, Mr. McCoy opened the door for me to become a partner. It had been a major financial stretch, but the opportunity was too attractive to pass by. More than that, it represented the fulfillment of a lifetime goal. I didn't have to think at all about whether to say yes. I'd been thinking about it my whole life.

I had just had another such moment, choosing to buy out and continue the Colley/McCoy Company as my own. But this presented another opportunity, one not so obvious. I could offer my son, Sal, the same opportunity Mr. McCoy had given me.

I could offer to sell him a stake and become a partner, too. We would own it together, father and son.

Sal said yes, happily and gratefully, as I had.

From there, things moved quickly. Mr. McCoy was very helpful with the many moving parts of the transition. He also smoothed the way with the McDonald's corporate office to secure approval of shifting ownership from his partnership to mine. We were following the 1994 model. Just as I became director of operations for the new company back then, Sal would assume the role in this new partnership, operating the restaurants. But there was another part of 1994 we had to go through that was not so pleasant. When I bought in, I had to mortgage or sell everything I owned to come up with the payment. Sal did the same thing, and he ran into the same problem I had: after everything he owned was "in the pot," he was still short. We continued working from the old playbook. Sal took his request to a large regional bank, only this time I played the role that Mr. McCoy had played for me. Unfortunately, we got the same outcome. The only difference was semantics: the banker, in a phrase I hadn't heard too often, told us that "the deal had no legs." He wouldn't make the loan.

Yet the 1994 replay wasn't all bad. After a few phone calls, further rearranging of finances, and the leveraging, again like before, not of assets but of character, reputation, and common sense, Sal was able to secure the money he needed. He was now a part owner, following the path I had taken, right down to the declined loan and the last-minute salvation.

As we were closing the transaction, I recall working on a press release with the corporate office. With 73 restaurants, we were one of the largest McDonald's operations. We needed to get the word out to other owner-operators, and we wanted to give the press a way to contact us if they reported on it, a major transaction in the regional economy. In those days, the Napoli group was still an acolyte of the fax machine – we had yet to do everything via email, as we do now. I recall sitting at home with Denise, watching the fax machine receive message after message of inquiry or congratulation.

We both had tears of joy down our faces. It was official: our son would carry on the family business, the one I had begun and he had already helped build. Denise and I could not have been prouder.

Then again, I also remember sitting in a conference room with Peter and David Sorgi, the father-and-son team that represented us as our attorneys. Peter turned to me and said, "From now on, when you and Sal wake up in the morning, you have to come up with an extra amount of money every day." For a moment, my excitement was replaced with the need to throw up out of nervousness! But I'm kidding – a little. Of course, Sal and I were able to meet the daily obligations and more.

* * *

There's a wall in our offices that records this event and pretty much every other big event in our lives.

It's a mural from ceiling to floor.

The mural is in the form of a tree, but it's also a timeline. My business life and my personal life are so intertwined – I really do think of the people I work with as family – that on this mural you'll find personal and professional achievements all mixed together. A milestone opening of a new Napoli Group McDonald's restaurant might be sandwiched between a wedding and the birth of another grandchild. Why not? Everyone I know and love is wrapped up in all of it. That wonderful mural is a daily reminder of all the highs we've come through and of how fortunate and blessed I've been – and we've all been.

There had been so many exciting moments to this point in my life, and once again we were at a "best ever" event, the latest great thing topping them all one more time: we were an independent family business – and I was partners with my son.

Executive conference room wall.

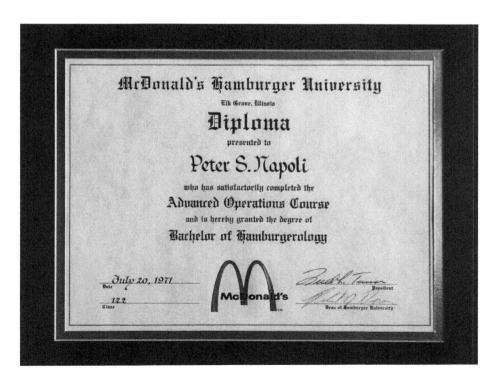

My first work permit.

Grand opening of my first restaurant as owner in Ayer, MA.

Celebrating the grand opening of our first McDonald's restaurant in Ayer, MA. My parents were beaming with pride.

Ronald, with Sal and myself, helping us celebrate Play Place's grand opening.

At the Townsend grand opening – our second McDonald's opening – with Melissa and Tina.

Sampling tasty food with
Ronald McDonald.

Helping with final cleanup
prior to the Concord III grand
opening.

Lynne and I recognizing our team at a summer outing.

Denise, Melissa, and Tina helping us celebrate Play Place's grand opening.

McDonald's CEO, Fred Turner, visiting one of our restaurants.

Denise and I, with friends, visiting with McDonald's founder Ray Kroc and CEO Fred Turner in Toronto, CA.

Receiving an award from the Leominster Chamber.

Giving a tour to City of Fitchburg officials.

Ronald stops by the house for a visit for Tina's birthday.

Sal and his team break the national drive-thru record.

"Mr. Hamburger" of Ayer

By Don Ogier

If a McDonald fanchise ever opens in Tiepraperzia (in central Sicily), native son Peter Napoli, guarantees that he'll be at the grand opening.

Thirteen when he and his family immigrated to this country, Peter Napoli is now the owner/operator of the Ayer franchise of the McDonald's Restaurant which will be opening at the rotary around December 1. While attending his first breakfast meeting of the Ayer Chamber of Commerce last Thursday he was warmly greeted and showered with best wishes. Colonel Richard Kattar, the featured speaker at the Devens hosted event, welcomed the "competition", as he called it, terming it a much needed facility for the area and for his troops - and a healthy competition for his food services at the Fort. Afterwards Napoli received promises from several in attendance that they would be at the rotary on opening day. Indeed, some confessed they'd been waiting years for the event.

Napoli is a product of the McDonald organization. He started with them as a counter man at the John Fitch store in Fitchburg in 1967 while he was attending Leominster High School, and became a shift manager at the Leominster store when he graduated from high school in 1969. The owner of the Fitchburg and Leominster franchises, then as now, was Rick McCoy, and Napoli has been with him ever since, working his way up to senior district supervisor (since 1980) of the four McCoy franchises in Leominster, Fitchburg, Gardner and Keene, N.H., as well as a portion of McCoy's Boston operation. In all, McCoy has 38 McDonald franchises - ten of them in New York.

The McDonald advancement program relies upon the talents and enthusiasm of inhouse staff. Consequently, Napoli has first hand experience with nearly every phase of the store operation which he now supervises with weekly visits, staff meetings and directives.

He remembers 15 cent hamburgers and a marquee number quite a bit lower than the 40 billion plus number that will be gracing his Ayer store. Another number that has changed is the franchise price. $350,000 is the

Peter Napoli

approximate cost that he and co-owner Rick McCoy had to put up for the Ayer store.

Napoli is a modest man and he credits McCoy for much of his success. He will continue to serve McCoy in a regional supervisory capacity and can't imagine not working for him. He is grateful for the opportunity to buy in with McCoy, an offer that McCoy extended to him in recognition of fifteen years of dedicated and proficient service.

Peter Napoli will no doubt be very visible at the Ayer McDonalds when it opens on December 1 (projected date); and no doubt he will be a familiar sight to many from this area who remember him as a counter man back in the sixties.

A resident of Leominster for 19 years, he resides in the Whalom District with his wife Denise and his three children who attend St. Bernard's Elementary School.

Newspaper publisher Frank Hartnett Sr. and his son were great promoters of business and were welcoming of our new restaurant.

AYER — Pictured left to right are Lee Guercio, Peter Napoli - speaker and Richard Maiore - program chairman.

MacDonalds speaker at Rotary

AYER — Peter Napoli, owner of the new MacDonalds in Ayer, spoke to the Ayer Rotary Club concerning MacDonalds history and operation.

Mr. Napoli pointed out that MacDonalds is 27 years old, and the MacDonald brothers are from Manchester, N.H. and moved to California where they went into business. Ray Crocker, a supplier of milk shake mixes, was impressed with their operation and went into business with them and was responsible for their branching out.

Mr. Napoli began his career in the Fitchburg MacDonalds #466, and Ayer will be #6500. MacDonalds stresses quality, service, cleanliness, courtesy. Each operation is expected to do over $1,000,000 in sales per year, and employees are given an opportunity to buy into the company. Opening date for Ayer is December 1, 1982.

A question and answer period followed the interesting talk.

Peter Napoli speaking at Rotary in Ayer, MA. (Karen Bobotas/Photographer)

McDonald's Comes to Ayer -
Aims for Perfection

By Charles Gordon

NEW MCDONALD'S................at Ayer's Markham Circle takes shape rapidly. Gordon photo.

AYER - "I'm going to work very hard to make it a showcase," Co-owner Peter Napoli of the now being built Ayer franchise of McDonald's Restaurant says as he oversees construction work at the Markham Traffic Circle site.

Even with a team of supervisors from McDonald's on site, Napoli views developments at the rotary on a daily basis. He has advised the landscaper to see grounds work done at a new McDonald's in Worcester in order to get some ideas for Ayer.

Already he can visualize the spacious finished structure. As he leads one around to show the layout of the place, he makes one sense that what he enjoys is the bustle of the staff as they fill orders and his personal contact with customers. In turn he is gratified by the number of people who have approached him to welcome him and his business to the area.

The seating capacity will be 105 persons, he says. Yet with all the spaciousness of the dining area he emphasizes that the place will be "comfortable and cozy." Three large bow windows will help make the place "open and light." He is enthusiastic as he points out the drive-through booth, the crew break area, the food storage section. Each franchise has its own points of individual uniqueness and takes on the latest in food storing and preparing equipment.

The hours for this restaurant will be 7 a.m. to 11 p.m. Sunday through Thursday and 7 a.m. to midnight on Friday and Saturday. He will not set up longer hours because he wants this restaurant "to stay as a family business."

With a construction completion date of December 1st, Napoli says he may start to hire help possibly after November 10th. Once hired these new workers will obtain practice at operating McDonald's restaurants in Leominster or Fitchburg. The firm's training program for new help and means of motivating people once they are on board Napoli views as "excellent."

AN EXAMPLE

"The young people we hire are terrific all in all," Napoli states. He has first-hand knowledge of the McDonald's employees in the area over the years since he himself started 15 years ago as a counterman in the Fitchburg franchise on

John Fitch Highway and has been with McDonald's ever since. In fact, he himself is an inspiring example of a person who has risen up through the ranks, so to speak, to positions of increasing responsibility.

The story is as pleasing in a different way as that of his father who left the small town of Tieprasperzia in Sicily with his family in 1963 to come to live in America on the principle that there is "a little more of a future here." The family had lived in the very town, by the way, that Bull Run Restaurant innkeeper Lee Guercio's mother came from. The father had been a businessman in Sicily who had a sister in Arlington, Mass. "He took a hell of a gamble," Napoli said as he spoke of his dad's decision from the standpoint of the good fortune he had here in America.

Napoli himself came to America with no previous knowledge of the English language. He went on, though, to graduate from Leominster High School in 1969. During those years he was on the work crew at the John Fitch Highway McDonald's.

Then he became shift manager at the Leominster franchise, making sure that the food was prepared properly, the service was good, and the workers were carrying out their tasks nicely, at the ages of 18 and 19. Here he started working for owner Rick McCoy, who now has 38 McDonald franchises, and McCoy became his mentor. McCoy's ownings grew to extend through Massachusetts and New Hampshire and to include 10 franchises in New York state and one in Vermont.

The next step was assistant manager of the

PETER NAPOLI............co-owner of the Ayer McDonald's franchise now being built at the Markham Traffic Circle, talks to Times-Free Press reporter about the new business. Gordon photo.

Fitchburg restaurant, which McCoy had had a chance to buy when he bought into the Leominster franchise. Napoli had the opportunity to open different franchises for McCoy as the business expanded.

Store manager at Leominster was the next position Napoli held in the McCoy business.

Since 1980 Napoli has been senior field supervisor, overseeing operations at nine restaurants, four in this area and five in the Boston area. This position Napoli will retain. McCoy is co-owner with Napoli of the new Ayer franchise. The new owners plan to have a store manager to run the franchise -- a person who will be promoted from within the ranks of employees.

Napoli resides in the Whalom District of Leominster with his wife Denise and children Sal, 10; Tina, 5; and Melissa, 2 months. He is determined to become active in local Ayer affairs, has already joined the Ayer Chamber of Commerce.

Motorists traveling around the traffic rotary in Ayer have a new landmark to watch as it rapidly moves toward completion. They await the new food service in the area as eagerly as Co-owner Napoli awaits their coming in to eat at "his house."

Newspaper publisher Frank Hartnett Sr. and his son were great promoters of business and were welcoming of our new restaurant.

185

Three generations attending owner/operator convention. (above)

Grand reopening celebration.

Grand reopening of Essex Junction II, VT.

Melissa brings her second-grade class from East Boston for a fundraiser to our McDonald's in East Boston. (left)

Footsteps

Current Title: Managing Partner/Director of Operations

Sal, where did you grow up? Leominster, MA

What schools did you attend? St. Bernard's Elementary & High School and Northeastern University

What prepared you most for the massive responsibility of being Director of Operations of the large number of McDonald's restaurants owned by The Napoli Group? I would attribute my readiness to three things:

1. Growing up in the business and watching, learning and listening to my father in his every day interactions with customers, community members and co-workers.

2. Always having a strong desire and willingness to seek out successful business professionals as role models.

3. Graduating with Entrepreneurship Degree from Northeastern University. During my time at NU, I gained valuable work experience from my co-op jobs ranging from sales to real estate. Those experiences taught me a lot about the importance of treating people fairly and with respect.

Can you define your role at The Napoli Group? The simplest explanation is that I oversee the day-to-day operations for all of our restaurants.

Q&A with Sal Napoli
Second generation owner/operator of The Napoli Company

The Napoli family: (l-R) Peter with his daughter Melissa, wife Denise and son Sal.

harder than my father. It's inspiring to grow up around someone that dedicated.

We learned that you and your father recently won a prestigious McDonald's Award. Can you tell us about that? Every year, McDonald's recognizes one owner/op-

ment options today that I believe can fit into everyone's lifestyle. Items like our Premium Salads with Grilled Chicken, Fruit & Walnut Salads and Parfaits for parents and Happy Meals with White Meat Chicken McNuggets, Apple Dippers and milk jugs for kids. As the father of two young children, I notice that there aren't a lot of places that offer these healthy choices at a great value.

We will put you on the spot -- what is your favorite McDonald's meal? Well, for breakfast, I love the Egg McMuffin that is made with fresh English muffins and fresh eggs, which are cracked at the grill. My other favorite meal is the Southwest Grilled Chicken Salad with Newman's Own dressing and a bottled water. I eat this meal several days a week.

The Newman's Own Organics coffee appears to be a big hit. How did that come about? New England coffee consumers are a different breed than the rest of the country so we recognized the need for a coffee that fits their tastes. We joined forces with Green Mountain and Newman's Own Organics to create a blend that we feel addresses our customers' desires.

We know how busy you are in fact we understand you often work long hours. Why

or purchase a new restaurant(s)? Truthfully, we don't spend time focusing on growth. Instead, we aim to deliver the best experience for our customers. However, when and if an opportunity for expansion presents itself, we always keep an open mind.

Sal and I receiving the Ronald award.

Denise and I finished the Falmouth Road Race and helped Sal raise over $150,000 for the Ronald McDonald House.

Denise and I being recognized at Italia Unita in Boston.

We Are Changing Our Name . . .

THE NAPOLI GROUP, LLC

But Not Our Principles, Philosophies Or Standards

The Napoli Family
Pictured from left to right: Melissa, Cettina, Sabrina, Peter J., Peter S., Denise, Lucia, Sal

Formerly Colley/McCoy Management Co, LLC

August 1, 2003: The big day when we took over all 73 restaurants as senior partners of the joint venture we share with McDonald's. There had been so many exciting moments up to this point in my life – and, once again, we were at a "best ever" event, the latest great thing topping them all: we were an independent family business, and I was partners with my son. (left)

We are so fortunate to have the most dedicated, hard-working, and effective leaders in the industry.

At our awards dinner, Lynne receives her 35th year service award.

Governor Sununu joins us for lunch at our Concord, NH, restaurant.

I believe in being involved in the political process.

Attending Massachusetts Governor Romney fundraiser.

Attending a fundraiser with then Boston Mayor Walsh and friends.

PETER & DENISE,
You GUYS ARE THE BEST!   Clitton T. Sununu

Denise and I were invited to the Governor's mansion for a holiday celebration.

My office wall.

OUR LARGEST EXPANSION EVER (2004)

In 2004, Sal and I decided to purchase the Jim Benware Organization, adding 20 McDonald's restaurants to our portfolio. These outlets were primarily in the Burlington, Vermont, area but also included six restaurants across Lake Champlain in the Plattsburg, New York, area, extending to the Canadian border. Most owner-operators with more than one restaurant oversee no more than 6 or 7 facilities. A string of 20 is triple the size of a typical large chain. This would be a significant addition and a shift with lots of moving parts, but since we were prepared, we could act quickly.

When you know the issues, and you *know* that you know the issues, you can act without hesitation. With thousands affected immediately by our decisions, every choice has profound ramifications. A delay in reacting has consequences, too. Fast, wise, informed, and confident decisions that are correct – you can't do business without them.

At least you can't do business for long.

Whenever we added restaurants to our operation, there was never any hesitation. I knew we could handle whatever came along because our management is passionate about McDonald's, our employees, and our commitment to customer satisfaction. They are as passionate as those of us who founded the organization, and they are true leaders.

For those in our organization for whom this expansion was their first experience with multiple acquisitions and openings, the effort was like earning an MBA in restaurant management.

The key to expansion is always in the people, and this move would require a lot of them, but we couldn't just post new positions in the want-ads and tell them when to show up. We would need to choose carefully, then to conduct extensive training not only for new employees but also for the current ones, since the task of keeping up to date on training had fallen behind.

There was one other complication, and it was a big one: we would have to coordinate all this from 200 miles away. The new restaurants were more than three hours by car from us!

With all this in play, you don't have to have any experience in business to realize the breadth of the challenge we were facing. We took it on gladly, but that didn't make it any easier. (Part of why we took it on was *because* it was difficult.) This was going to require leadership different from what Sal and I had used before. We would have to think about more people, more interactions, and more planning. We had more elements than ever in play, and they had to stay on track at all times. We had an advantage up front in that Benware had a great team in place that was hungry for change and opportunity. That made the transition that much easier. But the rest would be up to us.

Our first decision was to overcome the problem of distance by eliminating it. We would operate these new restaurants from a separate office in Burlington, Vermont. Once on-site, our Vice President and Manager of Operations Bob McDougall organized and executed the work along with Sal and me. They carried out their work with the support of the entire Napoli Group management team, men and women so reliable it's easy to forget how hard they work. (That's why, whenever I can, I remind everybody of just how great they are.)

Bob got an apartment near the new restaurants. Sal and I took turns working in Burlington, each of us spending every other week to support the transition and to keep people-development on track. We didn't sit in meetings or some makeshift conference, and we didn't spend those days staring down at a desk. We spent every hour in the restaurants helping with whatever came up, working face to face with our new employees to help them do a great job satisfying our customers. These folks were hungry for change, and ready to learn. They wanted not less responsibility but more. We quickly discovered that they would be our secret weapon and a major component of our success. For that reason (and many more), we would take good care of them.

In a few months, we decided to expand our support system, starting by providing Bob with a few more hands to help with this huge task. We promoted Jeremy Hinton to operations manager. It proved to be an outstanding decision. Bob and Jeremy worked well together. Under their leadership, we aligned the supervision and management of the 20 restaurants. We quickly saw improvements. Bob and Jeremy worked together on training, motivation, and people development, producing measurable gains in every area, including customer satisfaction. To this day, Jeremy continues in his role as director of operations – and as our company president.

By the way, if you're waiting for the part of this book where I complain about working so much, you are going to be disappointed. I loved spending time in the area. So did Sal. The work didn't wear us out. We thrived on it. In fact, when we were living out of a hotel, we took it as a reason to spend even more of our time in our newly acquired restaurants talking to our managers and crew.

Do you want to know the truth? It was fun.

We even managed to turn the most basic obligations, such as getting a meal for ourselves, into an opportunity to cultivate our people and show our appreciation and commitment. Every night, we would take some of our leadership to dinner and continue the conversation. It built camaraderie, and we enjoyed getting to know people and seeing everything fall into place. Our team appreciated the time and attention from the new owners, and they saw that we cared enough to take on this job personally. We didn't farm things out. Still don't. These restaurants belonged to us now, and we aimed to see that they got off on the right foot.

* * *

You can't make these kinds of expansions – acquisitions of entire restaurant groups that are already significant operations – without the leadership to do it. There won't be time to learn as you go. The executives have to be ready to execute. The only way we could have reached the point at which we could do something like this was by retaining committed individuals with decades of experience. They understand not just business in general and not just the restaurant business in particular; they understand *our* restaurant business – and it is *our* business, not just mine and not just Sal's.

All that the company has achieved, we have achieved together. We couldn't have done it any other way. There's a sense of true family and sincere caring that comes through in every process, every decision, and nearly every conversation. Everybody feels it, and it motivates us in a way nothing else can. This is what makes our business so different from everyone else's.

People stay with us not just for months but for years and, in many cases, decades. I believe it's because the respect we have for them is something they experience. We act on it. We create a comfortable environment and opportunity for growth in compensation, responsibility, and professional satisfaction.

When it comes to a strong and effective workforce, longevity matters. We apply this principle at every level of employment. For instance, we may find ourselves reviewing compensation and performance for an entire team in a restaurant, and the consensus, quite often, is that we should pay some key member more per hour. When these requests come to Sal and me, our response is always "Absolutely." We want to keep them, we want them rewarded, and we want to do the right thing by the people who work with us and for us.

But there's something else going on with that: it allows us to bring those employees, especially crew members, into a deeper understanding of the importance of their role in the business.

They're not just cogs to replace or the latest face behind the fryer. An increase in compensation is usually the result of exceptional work.

That has profound, positive consequences.

When we raise compensation, we're not just rewarding strong performance. We're opening the door to more growth and opportunity for the individual. They've already seen that an improvement in performance on their part brings rewards. Now they see that it translates to increased quality throughout the restaurant. It causes many folks to think about what other next "step up" they might take. Successful people enjoy that feeling and seek more of it, so the result is often additional better service in the restaurant and more increases in sales. In other words, hard work breeds more hard work, and success breeds further success.

Bottom line: when we pay more for outstanding work, our employees who receive more learn quickly that they can – and should – match that increase with effort. This drives improvement all around. As their fluency in doing a job increases, they prepare themselves for a better future.

In that spirit, the Benware acquisition created lots of opportunities for our people and lots of promotions, all of which we celebrated. Sal and I love that part of the job, and we enjoy having these events for awards and recognitions. We put on lots of dinner celebrations to mark milestones of growth and success.

These days, Jeremy has taken that over, but fortunately, Sal and I still get to come to the parties.

One of our annual traditions for people working at the level of a restaurant manager and above is an awards dinner at a beautiful property. We put everyone up in a hotel so everyone can celebrate safely and have a party into the night. It's just fun to do.

Our secret sauce is that we promote people from within. Sal and I are especially proud that all our restaurant managers, supervisors, and senior leadership were promoted from the crew rank. How many other businesses can say that? Jeremy Hinton, now president and director of operations, started as a 15-year-old. So did Jim Bilodeau, director of training. Come to think of it, so did Vice President and Director of Human Resources Lynne Shields and Vice Presidents of Operations Bob McDougall, Dan Frazier, and Jason Shunk. They've been with us since they were in high school.

What a privilege to share the work over all these years with such dedicated women and men. Nothing overwhelms them or defeats them. I've never heard them say, "It can't be done." You want a can-do attitude? Turn to them. That's how they live and work. They're also models for the kind of leaders we look for to help others find their own success.

In addition, we work hard to match the skills and interests of our employees with new opportunities and even newly created positions. Lee Anderson was a restaurant manager, but we saw he had an ability in technology. Now he's in charge of technology for our entire company. Bob Benson was an area supervisor. We saw he was good with repairs and building maintenance, so now he's in charge of our 10-person service department for all of our restaurants, taking care of HVAC and our equipment, and even leading some building repairs. I'm proud of this. We all are.

One more time! It all comes down to people.

* * *

Sometimes people tell me – nicely – that I ought to rethink my approach. "Wouldn't it be good to bring in some outside leadership, some folks from beyond the organization? Don't you want to hear from some new blood?"

Whenever I hear that, I smile. Everyone I work with in senior management feels the same way I do about all this. We know that the people we depend on are as smart as they come and just as passionate and motivated today as the day they came into their position in management. I'm happy to have new people, but I don't need a fresh perspective to tell me what my experience has already shown me.

Our success isn't a matter of somebody's opinion. If you want to test your business plan, look at the results. We're the third-largest chain of McDonald's in America. There's no need for a new perspective if you're already knocking it out of the park. Thanks to our great leaders, we've been doing that for decades, and we continue to grow.

I'm confident about what we do and where we're headed. That's not only because I've seen it work. It's because of the leaders we have in place and the way we brought those leaders into the roles they play. At every level, we bring folks to new responsibilities because of how well they already do what they do. If you're doing a good job for us, you're already looking to the next thing even as you execute the current thing you do with excellence. We give them new roles and more responsibility so they can continue to produce and impress, bringing their skills and insights to bear on new challenges and opportunities.

If there is a set of characteristics that everyone on our team has, it is this: we understand the importance of dedication, the commitment to being effective, and the spirit of sharing responsibility and credit.

Of course, it happens sometimes that people decide to move on in their careers and go elsewhere. But that's fine with me because part of great management is the human factor. If someone loses their desire to pursue the thing they're doing, you help them figure out the right move. It could be that they just need support to find that enthusiasm once more. Then again, it could be that the business they're in really isn't the business they should be in. When that's the case, you arrive at a mutual understanding, and, frankly, it's better for everyone. People who aren't happy in their work aren't doing the best they can.

We all deserve to be happy in our work. Life is short, and if you're not in the right place, you should get in the right place. When someone moves on, I may be disappointed that I won't be working with them anymore, but that feeling doesn't compare to how pleased I am that they're going to the next thing they're looking for. I want people to have the opportunity to live their best life and have their most satisfying career. When they leave to pursue that, they take the good experience with them that they had with us. They also give us the freedom to fill their previous role with someone who wants to do what we have in mind. We can then give that new person the same opportunity to grow and succeed.

It's a win-win, for sure.

SUCCESS...AND GIVING BACK (2004–2010)

The 2004 expansion brought us to 93 restaurants, the most restaurants we have had before or since. Though the exact figures are closely held at the corporate level, the Napoli Group was and remains among the top 5 largest McDonald's chains in the United States, and near the top throughout the world. In 2004, we employed nearly 4,000 people. We're part of dozens of communities in a personal and fundamental way, and not only economically.

Which leads me to this:

There's a verse in the book of Luke: *To whom much is given, much is required.* You don't have to be religious to see the decency in holding yourself to that standard. If you want a better world, that's where it begins.

Throughout my career, I have made generosity and philanthropy a big part of our corporate mission. I've tried to live that way myself, too. I've also tried to do it quietly. There are plenty of people who've done more than I ever could. Let the attention go to them.

I want to shine a light on the wonderful folks in our organization who have been generous in so many ways. Let me give you a brief tour of what they've achieved and why it is so important to our company and our communities.

* * *

Organizations can finance and promote philanthropy, but it's the people who get up in the morning and make it happen. In every one of our McDonald's restaurants, our crew members, managers, and area supervisors sponsor local teams, organize and run charity events, and even make personal donations to local causes. It's a priority at the restaurant level because I decided from the beginning that this would be a significant part of our corporate mission. I can compromise on a lot, but not this. Our restaurants must be a significant and valuable part of the places we operate.

It's good business, sure, but if that's the only reason you're doing it, you're missing the point. Here's the whole thing, in the words of my father: do unto others, then forget about it.

When you see somebody in need, you do something about it. If you have more than they do, you have even more of an obligation. Maybe you give somebody a place to stay when they don't have a place to stay. Maybe you help them out with a little money, a favor, a phone call, or by making a useful connection. It could be a million things. But when you see somebody who needs kindness, be kind.

In politics, they talk about the need for programs to address this or that problem. We have to have such programs, but we wouldn't need as much if each of us made it our business to look after those around us. When you see somebody who needs something, make it your problem, too. Don't wait for the government or society or somebody else to step up. If you take action yourself, that's one less problem to solve, one less person suffering.

It comes back to you in waves. Here's how that begins: when you make someone else feel better, it'll make you feel better. It has certainly been that way for me.

* * *

Here's an example of what our wonderful folks have done. For about 25 years, starting when I was in partnership with Mr. McCoy, the Napoli Group has sponsored an award for the state of New Hampshire to recognize excellence in education, the idea being to encourage and support teachers and administrators. We own half the McDonald's restaurants in the state of New Hampshire, so I met with the owners of the other half and invited them to join us on this. There's something powerful about people getting together for a cause. If we can use the McDonald's name in addition to McDonald's resources for a good thing, we're going to do it.

Here's another: we are enthusiastic supporters of the Ronald McDonald House Charities. They partner with the corporate side of McDonald's and individual restaurants to provide support for families with sick children. Probably the best-known program of the charities is the Ronald McDonald House. There is surely one near you: they provide a place for families to live when they have children in a nearby hospital. If you need a place to stay while your son or daughter is receiving treatment, the Ronald McDonald House is there for you.

Recently, the Burlington, Vermont, Ronald McDonald House launched a fundraising campaign. The goal was to raise $2.5 million to buy the building they occupy and to modernize it so it would be more comfortable and useful to the families who stay there. We own 20 of the 36 McDonald's associated with this facility, so we decided to donate a percentage of Happy Meal sales from those restaurants to the campaign. This generated about $300,000, but then we decided to do more. The Napoli Group had done something, and now my wife and I wanted to do something as the Napoli family. Since good food has always been such a part of our lives and our Italian heritage, our thoughts naturally turned to how we might do something for the House in that vein. We "bought" the kitchen facilities for the House and had it named in memory of our four parents, complete with a plaque on the wall. Now, with a significant portion of the funding in place, I joined the leadership of the House to use that financial foundation as a platform to finish the job, seeking donations from those who could do big things. That's how we finished the job.

These things are central to our mission. If there is any pride in what we do, it is the pride of being able to return some of the kindness so many have shown us. The people we give back to have always made us feel welcome and continue to allow us to make a living as members of their communities.

I mentioned the employees and leaders who do this good work, so I'll mention that, from my position as owner of the company, it's important to show kindness to them, too. I've tried to create a business that has the qualities of a family. That means creating a comfortable, welcoming, fair, and safe environment for them to work in. It means paying them well – always above the industry average – and providing a path for them to acquire more responsibility and advance in the organization.

If you say your employees are like family, treat them that way. Many times, this is more talk than action. Make a list of the things your family will do for you versus what your boss will do for you. In most cases, you'll get two very different lists – and the one about your family will be a lot longer than the one about work.

I hope we've been the exception. When people look back at my life and my work "family," I want them to see that I was different and our company was different. If somebody has difficulties, I hope we've made them feel like family. I recall a time or two when someone who had been with us a long time was buying a home but came up a little short on the down payment. We gave them an interest-free loan and an additional bonus. If you truly believe that your company is a family, that's the kind of thing you do. There are other examples, but as I've written here, things like that are better done privately and quietly. Having helped folks is plenty of reward for me.

* * *

The year 2004 was a pinnacle of achievement, but more big things lay ahead. This journey to something bigger would begin with getting a little smaller.

Between 2005 and 2010, we closed several more underperforming satellite restaurants. Small-site locations are a good way to grow market share, but it doesn't work in every market. It didn't work for ours. It was difficult to motivate people who understood that sales weren't meeting expectations. It was also hard to appropriately compensate hardworking people when the operation wasn't working as well as it needed to, harder still when everybody knew it. As I've said, the key to a successful restaurant is to create three things: a comfortable environment, growth opportunities, and above-average compensation. We could deliver the first two, but the last, which matters so much, of course, just didn't make sense given revenues. We pulled the plug.

The effort had been a calculated risk, so I could accept the live-and-learn outcome. This closing would make room for a new opportunity. But what would it be? The answer came quickly.

BECOMING INDEPENDENT (2011–2019)

In 2011, McDonald's came to me with a proposal to dissolve our partnership.

They wanted to increase their number of corporate-owned restaurants. The Napoli restaurants were an obvious source for the expansion. At that time, we owned 87 restaurants in partnership with the corporation. These co-owned properties were exceptionally valuable, as sales were at an all-time high. A deal would be neither easy nor cheap for either side. They proposed keeping 28 of the restaurants and selling us their interest in the remaining 59.

This was an exciting opportunity. I would be sad to part with 28 restaurants in Massachusetts because this is where I had started, but my nostalgia was outweighed by three things. First, I respected McDonald's decision. We had come this far together by looking out not only for our own interests but also for each other's. Second, the split would create new opportunities for our people to be part of the iconic McDonald's brand. Sal and I had made our bones with McDonald's. This would open that door to other people who worked for us, people whose future we care about. Third, and this was the pinnacle, Sal and I understood that our buying out this part of the shared investment would be the fulfillment of another dream: creating a chain of Napoli-owned McDonald's across four states, 100 percent within our organization.

But could we pull it off?

* * *

We worked closely with executives at McDonald's headquarters to ensure we could make the transition at all, and, if we could, to make it as smooth as possible for everyone. One of our first priorities would be to use this moment to create opportunity for our people. The restaurant crew, managers, and team would stay with the restaurants regardless of ownership, so their jobs would remain. Their security was important to me. Area supervisors and operations managers could choose to join McDonald's corporate if an offer was forthcoming to them or to stay with what was poised to become the independent Napoli Group.

We were negotiating with McDonald's East Zone President Rick Colón, who oversaw this mammoth 4,000-restaurant element of the company and who, these days, is the COO of Dunkin' Brands, the donut people. Rick was and remains a great executive, a formidable advocate for company interests but also someone who wants the best for everyone involved. The 87 restaurants were valuable, and the price he asked for reflected it. Sal and I almost fell off our chairs when we heard the number.

You may wonder how we could have been so surprised since, sharing the restaurants, Rick's side and ours had identical access to financials and facts. It wasn't that we differed on the value of the restaurants in the here and now. We differed on what they would be worth over time. If you're selling, you're going to be as optimistic as you can reasonably be. If you're buying, you're going to tamp down that enthusiasm to keep a lid on the price. Businesses for sale are typically priced as a multiple of cash flow. Around this time, a standard valuation was five or perhaps six times cash flow. It could be even more based on assets, the outlook, taxes, and other obligations. A difference of opinion on all that was the source of our difference in price.

We were about $40 million apart, and Rick could tell that Sal and I were shocked. But what could have been an awkward or even messy encounter became just the next step in negotiation between reasonable individuals. In only a few more calls, we were both able to justify our valuations to the other. We remained separated by this eight-figure number, but at least we knew why, and that would be the basis for productive negotiation.

We would have to work through our differences restaurant by restaurant, and point by point. A typical example was a pair of restaurants in Maine. By retooling management, systems, and processes, Sal and I along with the Napoli team had increased cash flow significantly. We'd done it in record time, too: within only six months after we had purchased them earlier that year. But now McDonald's had doubled their valuation of these properties, despite their increased value having come solely from what we did. We didn't think that was fair, and we said so. And this was just two of the 55 we were working to acquire, never mind the valuations for the 28 McDonald's would keep for themselves. This negotiation, though collegial and between friendly partners, had the potential to be drawn out, bruising, and technical.

Sal and I were flying to Atlanta, Georgia, when we received a voicemail from Rick. He wanted to meet for lunch when we landed to continue our conversation and, if possible, come to an agreement. Sal and I liked the sound of that. But no matter how cordial the conversation, there would be no easy way to sweep all that calculation and analysis into a decision over a meal. Or was I wrong?

We sat down for lunch and the usual pleasantries – sincere, as always, but there was of course the elephant in the room. Lunch commenced. Both sides knew what we hoped we could achieve and how hard it would surely be to meet in the middle.

But I thought, *might as well try.*

I put down my fork and picked up a pen. I found a piece of paper and wrote down a number, a final dollar figure that was the product of the calculation Sal and I did and the great financial thinking our team had produced. But there was instinct at work as well. I knew what Rick wanted. Rick knew what I wanted. I slid my number across the table. It reflected the expectations of both sides: what we needed to have an independent future as the Napoli Group and what McDonald's needed to realize a profit in moving on without us.

Rick lifted the edge of the paper and glanced at the figure I'd written for him. He smiled and nodded. *Was it a nod of agreement or a nod of "you've got to be kidding"?*

"Okay, Peter. We have a deal," he said. And that was that.

Smiles came all around. Handshakes followed. We finished lunch together, relaxed, and happy. Generous servings of relief were enjoyed all around.

It was a pleasure to deal with Rick and with this big company, but it could have been a whole different story, at least if the cast of characters had been different. When you think of a deal like this, you assume it'll be lawyers and paperwork and formality, but McDonald's is a smart company with smart executives. They empower their leadership to make fair, smart deals. They don't demand endless rounds of reviews and legal eagles sitting on everyone's shoulder. At the end of the day, both McDonald's and my own company are people companies. That's a lot of why we've gotten along so well for so long and why the Napoli Group has become the third-largest owner-operator in the organization.

Not long after, we all signed the paperwork to make the deal official: we owned 59 restaurants entirely on our own.

* * *

As has often been the case in my life, a moment of great success was accompanied by profound sadness. In March 2011, my mother passed away at the age of 89.

She lived a good life and a long one – 89 years! How wonderful to have so many years with us all. She saw so many changes in the world and so many good things come to pass for her family. She shepherded us when we first came to America, taking care of the home front as we made our way – and of course, she worked a job outside the home. She got to see her children's successes, including my own, and the birth of many grandchildren. It's always sorrowful to lose a parent, but I took great satisfaction in the fact that she had a long and fulfilling life.

* * *

Soon after the acquisition, Sal and I were at a McDonald's convention where we ran into McDonald's USA President Jan Fields. The challenge of the deal was well known in the McDonald's C-suite, and I joked with her that if we had known a year before that they had been planning to dissolve the partnership, we would not have worked so hard to build sales and cash flow in restaurants we would soon buy back.

Her response was classic: "If you hadn't worked as hard as you did to build up those restaurants," she said, "we wouldn't have offered you 55 of them. We would have offered you 5!" Of course, she was right, and of course, Sal and I would never have done less than our best, regardless of what was down the road. To be honest, what we do is not just satisfying but also great fun. We wouldn't deny ourselves any of the pleasure of a job well done. Our hard work made more profit for everyone involved, starting with our team.

Of course, not everybody feels that way about the ratios that connect work, risk, and reward. I'll occasionally meet a managing partner who gives off a sense of "I don't know if I should work this hard since I'm not getting 100 percent of the return." I think that's dumb. You always give 100 percent – that's what a responsible person does. You always take your best shot. It's the mark of a true professional. If you're not giving your all, you're not a pro, and you won't be on my team for long. It's as simple as that.

Jan said our transaction had "made their year," meaning we were a major contributor to the corporate bottom line. We had achieved that by working for our interests as well, naturally, but the benefit accrued to both partners.

* * *

The burden we had taken on was scary, but Sal and I forged ahead. The first three years were difficult, and we were ready. My dad had taught me early and often to be ready for adversity by planning – and saving – for challenging times. He told me to set aside something for a downturn because there's always one to come.

With the help of our bankers at Bank of America, we came up with a financing package that would let us run the restaurants the way we wanted while meeting our obligations. Still, those first three years were tough. The year 2014 was especially hard. We couldn't make our obligations without dipping into our line of credit. We made no profit. Sal and I took nothing out of the company except for taxes. You can't run a business like that for long, but here's the thing: you can do it for a little while, especially if you understand why you're doing what you're doing, if you have a good idea of when the turbulence will end, and if you're committed to a plan based in reality.

We were working on something big. We were committed. We believed in what we were doing because we knew what we were doing. Hard times were built into the calculation.

Besides calling on lessons my father taught me, another portion of my confidence came from having already weathered storms in business. As a result, these tough times didn't send us into panic mode.

We knew up front it was going to demand sacrifice. That was acceptable because we had prepared for it mentally, financially, and in terms of management. Was there an easier path we could have taken? Sure. In fact, in 2011, I could have walked away with a pile of money and disappeared into the sunset, but that's not who I am. Then and now, I have a responsibility to help my son run our business, to look after my family, and to consider the interests of the many people in our organization who rely on what we do.

I'm pleased to say that all this turned out to be a great decision for us. It may sound a little prideful to say this, but I never doubted what we chose to do.

* * *

With this bigger business, now one of the largest McDonald's chains in the United States, Sal and I continued acting on one of our main philosophies of business: namely, maintaining your position is never enough. By 2015, the system was sound, and our resources were in place. Now we needed to bring in more smart, skilled individuals who shared our perspective on the sources of growth and success and who shared our commitment to helping others build a successful future for our organization and themselves.

Sal and I reorganized leadership to include a new position,

president and director of operations, which would be awarded to Jeremy Hinton. Again, there was temptation to overcome. It would have been easier to cut management, skip elevating Jeremy, and put Sal in the new position. We could have cut other senior positions and pushed everything and everybody to do a little more and just carried on.

But that's not how we do business. It's not right, and it doesn't work.

Sal and I kept our eyes on the bigger picture: what would build sales, profit, and cash flow? We wanted to build for the future by developing our people, ensuring customer satisfaction, marketing our business, expanding sales, training our people, and developing whatever new skills we might soon find that we needed. This was a smart play, and obviously, it paid off. It left Sal and me lots of time to plan, direct, and motivate, as well as to spend time in our restaurants. I look back at this with special pride.

This was a pivotal point in our history and in our success. We overcame hardship. We emerged stronger. We took on 55 restaurants and made a stronger operation at the same time.

Through our hard work and perseverance, we emerged from challenge and change at the pinnacle of achievement – the result of a dream I shared with my son, my family, and my team, and the success of a lifetime.

Nice Country, America!

224

THE COVID SOLUTION (2020–2022)

The way I see it, a *problem* is something you can resolve with your efforts, at least somewhat. But a *difficulty* is different: it's a thing that's out of your control.

Like those times when you go to the doctor and there's nothing they can do but send you home to take aspirin, some difficulties are beyond your capacity to change. Over my years in business, I've seen a few: gas shortages, supply-chain-food shortages, runaway inflation, and an employment market so tight that it was a challenge to staff our restaurants.

Whether it's a problem or a difficulty, you have to get out in front of it before a cascade of other issues follows. With planning and hard work, you can avoid some of them, but when they originate from an out-of-your-hands *difficulty*, the challenge increases by orders of magnitude. You'll have to work harder, smarter, and longer. You may not be able to resolve the original issue, but you can limit the further trouble it can cause. That's what leaders do.

Like dominoes falling, the results of one nearly intractable difficulty can have a long reach. I remember those gas shortages of the 1970s causing not only high fuel prices but also empty tanks underneath the filling stations themselves. That was the first falling domino, and it led to increased prices for everything, which fed already-roaring inflation. You can look at the situation in recent months and years for examples of how high gas prices are once again wreaking havoc.

The reason is obvious: at some point, everything in our lives relies on transportation. When this problem happened in the 1970s, our costs for the restaurants went through the roof. That meant low-to-no profit for a while – and the dominoes started to fall. With slashed profits and even losses, it was a challenge – and occasionally impossible – to meet basic obligations such as loan repayment and payroll.

For a company committed to paying wages above the industry average, that payroll problem came with trouble all its own. We have always been committed to treating our people not just right but well. Hard times don't change that because, to us, it's not just a nice idea but a promise – and that's good business. By committing to compensate our people well, we naturally commit to running a business whose products and services are uniquely attractive to the public. But if you can't afford the staff you need and the cost of food is rising, the dominoes fall faster and faster, making excellence harder to achieve.

When all this happened in the 1970s, I wasn't yet an owner. I was watching from the ranks of the managers and employees – though I conducted myself as if I owned the restaurant. It was good experience because I got to think through not just a problem but a true difficulty, something out of my hands. I learned from Mr. McCoy and the leadership of the Colley/McCoy Company how to come through a crisis.

I'm glad I banked the experience because, almost fifty years later,

I faced a crisis of my own.

* * *

I've been around a bit. I've seen a lot of things. And I'm not exaggerating when I say that March 2020 brought the most traumatic experience of my life.

The onset of the Covid lockdowns and all the anxiety, fear, and risk that came with them reminded me of the stories of world-changing events I heard from my parents and grandparents. They had told me about being in Sicily during World War II as the Allies were invading the country in Operation Husky in 1943, the first phase of the Italian campaign. Every man, including my father, was conscripted into service and sent to war. Suddenly living in an occupied country, the family had food only because my grandfather had a farm.

No, Covid wasn't World War II, but it was still a battle and would come with human casualties and economic strife that would affect the quality of life for millions of Americans, and that of billions of people around the world.

As we listened to news about the pandemic, we were concerned about contracting the disease, but that wasn't our biggest worry. There were already ways to limit exposure, and early treatments for infection had appeared. A vaccine was on the way, too. The big concern was not so much the fatality rate, which was fairly low unless you had comorbidities, but the problem of needing a hospital bed and finding they were already filled. So Covid was a threat but not the only one. It wasn't even what worried us most.

Our greatest fear was that we might be ordered to shutter our business, leading to the end of our decades-old family enterprise. Not only would that foreclose on the purpose it had given our lives, but it would also eliminate the foundation it has provided for so many people, neighborhoods, and communities. In this way, the "difficulty" of the pandemic was set to yield yet another problem that would be out of our hands: the government severely constraining how we would be allowed to respond. In the frenzy of those days, when shouting "believe the science" became a bullying substitute for actually knowing that something was true, we feared the unappealable and likely less-than-informed declaration of an elected official or bureaucrat that businesses would have to close. Such an order could have come at any minute, with no consideration for competing interests and no avenue for challenge.

For a while, every entrepreneur in America was at the mercy of essentially unchecked economic authority at the federal, state, and local levels. Authorities, both elected and unelected, had taken it upon themselves to make the biggest decision in US economic history: namely, that we might be forbidden from participating in choosing our risk tolerance and that our free-market enterprises might be closed down and perhaps bankrupted – but, somehow, it would be "for our safety."

You know how I feel about choosing my risks. You also know the obligation I carry for my community and the country that I love. I care about looking out for the employees who rely on me. This wasn't a decision to be made lightly by anyone, yet the rights of citizens and economic actors seemed an afterthought to those who would decide. But there was one thing we could do: we could decide how to conduct ourselves in response to whatever came, despite restrictions that could be put in our way.

As feared, the lockdowns came in forms both official and unofficial. Some businesses were shuttered indirectly because of restrictions on comings and goings. Others were allowed to remain in operation but with commerce so limited by social pressures that they might have been formally closed anyway. "Two weeks to flatten the curve" became two months and ultimately more than two years of limits, pressures, and assertions of authority made quickly and capriciously, sometimes with a public justification of "science" but more often based on whatever pre-published paper or popular declaration that happened to grab a reporter's attention. Even these iron-clad edicts were rapidly swapped out, changed, or withdrawn, perhaps to avoid becoming a "live" issue that would allow them to be challenged in court. This was the situation we faced as winter ended in 2020.

Despite all that, we had a few things on our side, starting with the fact that we were in an excellent financial situation with little debt. Still, if the registers stopped ringing, we would quickly be in a world of hurt. All we knew for sure was that, come what may, we would keep our people working wherever possible and compensated as long as we were able. We would continue to attend to the things that matter most to us: our employees and our communities. I insisted we keep our commitment, and my leadership team stood shoulder to shoulder with me.

As this roller-coaster ride began, my son, Sal, stepped up. "Dad," he said, "you brought us to this point. I will take it from here." So I'll let him share the story, then I'll hand it off to the rest of the senior leadership team to get everybody's perspective on those intense days.

* * *

Sal Napoli: "You brought us this far, Dad. I'll take it from here." I vividly recall making that statement. I also remember in that moment having an unbelievable level of confidence in our ability to do what we were about to attempt.

You have to remember, the world economy was already in free fall, and that was just at the outset. Nobody had any idea what the ultimate effect of Covid-19 would be on business in general and certainly not on ours in particular. Still, I was confident because of what my father taught me and the example he set for me and all of us throughout our lives. If I had to sum it up in a phrase, I'd choose this one: we solve problems. That's one thing I know for sure: we solve problems, big ones and small ones, every day of the week.

Big problems need detailed plans, so that's what we assembled. We called it "Operation Build Up," and it was a direct reflection of my father's leadership and foundation. It was the application of just about every principle he has followed, and the expression of every mission we hold dear.

We weren't there just to survive, either. We came to thrive.

In the face of so much uncertainty, Jeremy Hinton, our president and director of operations, Lynne Shields, our vice president, and Jim Thomas, also a vice president as well as our chief financial officer, immediately implemented this plan. They came with a positive approach and pushed away all distractions. Everything was on the line, and they treated it like that, and they did not allow themselves to be distracted by all that was at stake. This is to say that in the best tradition of my father's style of management, they focused not on the problem but on the many solutions we would need.

When a crisis arises, the foundation for a response has to be in place already. Ours was there because the core of my dad's leadership has always been the importance of relationships, a commitment to treating people fairly and with respect, exhibiting confidence, and keeping our eyes not on the problem but on the answer.

We have the best people in the business, starting with our senior leadership. I knew I could count on their "own it" mentality. In return, they deserved to know that I stood behind them. Therefore, I told them this explicitly: whatever the outcome, I take responsibility. Don't worry that anyone here will blame you if, somehow, we don't succeed. If that happens, I take the blame. But if, as I expect, we succeed, the credit goes not to me but to you and all of us.

For the first several months of Covid, all decisions went through me, sometimes as a participant and sometimes just for approval and monitoring. I'm not usually involved in every decision at every level, but these were unique times, and we needed one person to have an eye on the whole picture.

Nobody worked from home. I was in our office for 30 days straight, many times leaving after 11 pm, and walking out to the parking lot next to Jim. The whole team was there with us pushing through, days, nights, and weekends. Too many people were depending on us to not do anything less.

* * *

Within 24 hours of the first restrictions, Jeremy set up a call with our operations team. This was vital because we needed to set the tone for all that would follow. I wanted them to have absolute assurance that we were working to preserve their jobs and the company itself. It was imperative that they felt a strong bond of trust with us in a time when certainty was in short supply. I'm proud to say this major task wasn't difficult at all. The way we had run the business from Day One, the relationships were already strong, and the trust was already there. This wasn't an exercise in persuasion. It was a reminder among colleagues in a crisis that the trust remains. I learned long ago from my father that "happy talk" is never enough, especially in tough times. People deserve specifics. It's how they know you're "real." That is, they need to know not just that you're going to make good decisions, but how you're going to make good decisions. They needed us to explain ourselves, and we did.

We stated plainly that their wellbeing was our priority and that every choice we made would be made in light of these things: we would demonstrate leadership, we would make clear our trust in them and each other, we would always show respect and act in fair and reasonable ways, and we would stay committed to finding solutions and quickly turning ideas into action.

This was nothing new for them to hear us say. The problem was new, but our approach was the same as always, rock steady, and predictable as sunrise: responsibility, trust, and commitment.

A company exists to make money, closely followed by taking steps to make sure it's still in business tomorrow. For a while, our focus would not be on making money but on making it through – but not at all costs. We would ride this out by contributing to our communities, showing compassion for our customers, and being a safe place for our employees. To maintain your position, you have to keep growing, but now we would have to maintain just by maintaining. The only question was how long we could keep it up – hopefully longer than the pandemic, or at least long enough for a measure of proportion and reality to return to those making the rules from on high.

One of the first things we did was to secure personal protective equipment (PPE) for everyone. We did this so quickly that we had our PPE before McDonald's corporate headquarters had addressed the issue. Of course, in those early days, finding PPE was not a trivial matter. Most of us didn't even know what the words meant. But as leaders, it was our job not to puzzle over the problem but to dig in to find what our people needed. I went through all my contacts until I came across the contact information for one of my high-school classmates. Their family owned a large chain of hardware stores. I made a call to explain what we needed, and, just like that, we secured masks and gloves for all our people. They were pleased to help us, and I drove over myself and crammed the first bundle in my car.

Around the same time, Jim reached out to our banking partners at Enterprise and Fidelity along with the company that administers our payroll. The question was simple: what can you do to keep payroll on track, and is there anything we can do to support you?

Meanwhile, Lynne and Jeremy took the lead to implement Operation Build Up, which included not only a step-by-step plan but also a first-draft list of the questions and problems we anticipated would arise across 66 restaurants with 10 area supervisors and 66 general managers. It was a commonsense approach: when a problem appeared, we'd check the plan for an answer, and if there wasn't one we'd figure it out and add it, growing and refining the plan while we implemented it. This ever-evolving document would turn out to be the most effective tool we had.

Also in those first 48 hours, we performed a complete financial analysis – what might happen and what the results might be – so we could do practical planning. We projected restaurant-by-restaurant sales as well as overall company numbers for decreases in business of 30 percent, 40 percent, 50 percent, and beyond. With new income ceilings for worst-case scenarios, we dissected literally every line on the profit and loss statement to find potential savings – and not just the largest items such as labor and food cost. We didn't keep anything off the chopping block. The question was simple: what could we trim or do without and still maintain the excellence we demand, but within these new limits?

The best way to appreciate how we made these decisions is to think about what you might have done in your own home. We reduced the frequency of trash pick-up. We cut back and sometimes eliminated window cleaning. We canceled subscriptions to lobby-music services. We cut landscaping to the bare minimum. If we could stretch a good or service a little, we'd stretch it, and if we could do without it, it was gone. The idea, of course, was to find a way to function so we could still pay our employees and meet our standards of high-quality service and food.

But there's also this: during this massive downturn, we maintained incentives for our employees and re-engineered them so they were still constructive and attractive in this drastically different environment. That's how much our employees mean to us. We wanted them to know that, and we wanted to do more than just say nice things. We wanted to give them something they could use at a time when many needed help more than ever.

Some McDonald's here and abroad closed up shop and sent everybody home. Some had to take a hard look at just how much they were willing to prioritize, de-prioritize, and sacrifice in support of their employees set against what they could do and still be confident the business would survive the pandemic. As long as we were allowed by the government to make our own responsible choices, we chose to support our employees and our community with work, opportunity, and generosity. I'm proud that we did. That core plan we formed in the first four days was pretty much the plan we followed through the entire pandemic, and we still use elements of it today for their thrift and efficiency.

We kept a massive organization aligned. We stayed positive. We not only maintained but grew the respect our teams have for our leadership, and our respect for them grew with it. Though we knew this at the outset, we saw the absolute truth of the power of relationships: every second we spent showing every employee that they are valued and appreciated was a second well spent.

* * *

One of the things that helped me personally was a new routine that brought information, confidence, and camaraderie to my decision-making: daily conference calls with other owner-operators across the country. We shared insights, problems, and things we'd learned both to avoid and to implement. Some days, I would just listen and others I would share something I knew could help everyone else. I gained a lot of knowledge this way, and it helped me to push through knowing that there were many of us out there seeing so many of the same successes and challenges. I don't think there was any call that didn't give me at least one little nugget that was helpful to our organization.

That was matched with the constant communication I had with our senior leadership team, our supervisors, our operations managers, our general managers, our service department and support staff, plus our training, technology, and finance departments – everyone in the Napoli Group, and that goes for everybody. If you were on our payroll in this time at our restaurants or here at our main office, you have my gratitude and my respect, no exceptions. My colleagues were beyond tremendous and amazing.

This business-as-family quality was at the center of our success. We began with the foundation of commitment to others and responsibility for the burdens we assume: this my father instilled in all of us, and we were better able to act on that because of the experience we've had over the years, the trust we have in each other, and of course a willingness by everyone involved to work hard and work smart. There would have been no success in this crisis without the amazing leadership of our operations managers, our supervisors, our general managers, our crews, and our entire service department and support staff, including our training, technology, and finance department. We had the experience and the skills from the outset. The job over these last couple of years has been to keep doing what we do best, to solve problems. And that's what we have done.

* * *

Lynne Shields: I'll second what Sal said. You know what brought us through? Calm, focused, attention to detail, and a well-thought-out approach by leadership. With that in place, everyone who depended on the leadership team could do their jobs with confidence. If there was any inner turmoil in this group, no one made a show of it, and no one let their concerns spook anybody else. We weren't going to let the situation define how we handled it. We were going to define how we handled the situation.

My favorite example of getting out in front of things? Sal wasn't going to wait for McDonald's on the PPE. He called a friend from high school then went over to one of their stores and loaded the stuff in his car!

Then there's this: as he said, communication outside our world was critical. There were video conferences with people from national, regional, and local positions, and they'd cover every topic under the sun, from PPE to the latest from the CDC – a real alphabet soup of sources, ideas, and experts. At first, it was like drinking from a firehose. Any of us could have made the case that we should just drop off the calls and go it alone, especially because we were crazily busy. I credit Jeremy for making what felt like a tangled mess into a well-ordered resource. He burned the midnight oil to create a practical inventory of who the experts were on any given topic. With that, we could assign questions and assignments more effectively, and we knew who was responsible for any given thing, including the high, hard ones. Efficient communication makes all the difference.

* * *

Jeremy Hinton: Lynne, thanks for that, but of course, we could tell a story about what everyone here did that we couldn't have gotten along without. That tells you a lot about the thing that surprises me most, though it shouldn't surprise me at all. We created a lot of powerful management systems for just those difficult times that proved so flexible that we're going to keep a lot of them as part of how we do things from now on. That reflects the beauty of the Napoli Group: even in a crisis, we stay true to our core. The result is that the things we do in any given situation are far more likely to have application in a lot of other settings. In this way, we're naturally oriented toward smart evolution.

The character of any company is the character of its leaders. It shows in far more than big-picture decisions. I like to point at "boots on the ground" things, and a couple of them make this clear.

The first was to support customers and the community: we kept the bathrooms open. Most McDonald's locked the doors and went strictly with the drive-thru. Not us. We left our doors open. You couldn't order at the counter, but if you needed a restroom, you could use ours. It sounds like a small thing until you're out and about and everything's closed and suddenly you need a bathroom!

The second was for our employees. Long before it became a more common practice across the McDonald's system, we let our employees eat free during their shifts. When the pandemic hit, this became more than just a perk. Suddenly, many of our employees had become one-income families. This was a thing we could do that would help in a tangible way. We wanted to reassure our people that we would support them. It was the right thing to do.

We had two competing interests that we chose to make complementary. We were committed to providing tangible support for our employees and our communities, and we were committed to ensuring that the business would still be standing when all this was over. To thread that needle, we set aside the profit priority. Losses would be not just acceptable but a wise trade – if that meant we would still be around when the music stopped.

I'm proud that the Napoli Group leadership is the same today as it was when this began in March 2020. We stuck together out of loyalty to this shared enterprise, to each other, and of course to Peter and Sal. They've stood by us, and this was a time when we needed to stand by them. And we stood together – as we always had. What an honor to be a part of that.

* * *

Jim Thomas: What stood out to me was the calmness that everybody had, especially Peter and Sal. Lynne kept us apprised of the resources we had, and new government programs as well. If Jeremy was stressed he never showed it. Everyone in leadership inspired everyone else to be confident. They were nothing but supportive. I was grateful.

The shutdowns, when they came, turned into far more than the original assurances, as we all now know. The first was supposed to be no more than 8 weeks, then it was 24 weeks, and then it was through the end of 2020. So, everyone had to be flexible, sort of planning for the worst, hoping for the best, then getting in sight of the promised relief only to watch somebody move the goalposts and change the rules of the game.

As Chief Financial Officer, I was heavily engaged with the Paycheck Protection Program, better known as PPP, plus all the technical and managerial decisions it took to make sure we were paying our bills, getting paychecks to our employees, maintaining financial incentives in a time when they were especially important, and keeping the company in a solid position when it comes to debt, dollars, and cents. I thought about all this as three intertwined concerns: customer care, employee morale, and cutting profits for the sake of the people who depend on us but maintaining the income we would need to stay in business.

Every day, both here at headquarters and in the stores, we worked hard to restore a little bit of normalcy. That meant we didn't stay home. We came in. That turned out to be important because you

can't just declare things are normal. You have to do the things –
the safe things – you can to help people feel confidence and see
competence. We're a big company, but I saw close-up that we can
move pretty quickly when we need to.

It's funny, looking back. We had to do so much so fast – those
years seemed like a long time and a short time at the same time.

Jeremy: We operate in four states, so we were dealing with
direction, especially at the outset, from McDonald's, the federal
government, and four states – sometimes in conflict. It took this
whole management team working together to get to the right
answer.

Then there was the speed things changed: from March to April
we went from 2,400 employees down to a little over 1,700, and
by summer we were back to where we started. There were a
lot of factors in that. For example, 40 percent of our employees
are under 18. With so many unknowns, some parents weren't
comfortable letting their kids work. On the other end of the
spectrum, we have older people who understood the unique
threat that Covid seemed to pose to people approaching or in
their retirement years. Plus, some people lived with someone with
a health-related issue. We respected everyone's personal decision
on whether to work, and we went way beyond the extra mile to
create a safe environment that inspired confidence. It wasn't long
before we were welcoming many of them back. Eventually, we
returned to recruiting, which included incentives.

Lynne: Those are decisions with a lot of moving parts, so you
need data to make those choices. I don't think we can emphasize

enough the reliability that we made sure we had. When it came to Covid risk, Jeremy and the team left nothing to chance. I'm sure he treated our employees and executives with the same caution and concern he used with his own family. We had travel protocols. We had a deep cleaning team that would go in. We had consistency in protocol and expectation across every restaurant we owned. That transparency and reliability built confidence at every level.

These individuals made themselves visible in the restaurants – which was nothing new, of course. That's what we've all done from the start. But now it took on greater meaning. They were just as approachable and available as they had always been. During the first couple of spikes in cases, it made all the difference in the world. Nobody ran. Nobody hid. Nobody had one set of rules for themselves and a stricter set for others. They put on the gloves and the mask and went to work.

We kept a rolling, 14-day average of identified cases. That first summer, this number never got above 10.

Sal: What we learned in that first wave, along with what scientists and doctors provided, made the second wave a lot easier to deal with, and a whole lot safer.

If someone tests positive anywhere in the operation, it's communicated to this office in real-time. In fact, I saw that Jeremy received just such a text as we've been sitting here talking. That's how we set it up at the start, and that's how we do it today.

Jeremy: We had a bit of a secret weapon in the McDonald's system.

Our business was already 70 percent in the drive-thru, and we had just introduced delivery. I hadn't thought delivery would be a big thing for us with the average check in our industry, but Covid made delivery a very big deal and a significant and fresh way to support our customers. Then we had digital sales and mobile interactive, so we were better prepared than most.

* * *

Now, back to me, Peter, to wrap up.

For me, the best takeaway from all this is simple: if you were there at the beginning, you were still employed at the end. We didn't fire or lay off a single person during the pandemic. Of course, some people needed to be home with children, so they chose to take unemployment instead of a leave of absence so they could receive compensation from the state and federal governments. We understood that, and of course, we would welcome them back if they decided to return. There were other reasons, too. Some people wanted to take the time off, pursue some other interest, or try some other job, and of course, we are happy for people to do what they want to do. At the height of things, we had as many as 300 people take a leave. But many of these folks had been with us a long time – they were, as I've said, a part of the family. So, for many folks, we sent them notes around the holidays, sent them meal-for-two cards, and reminded them that their job was still waiting for them if they decided to come back. A lot of them did!

Thanks to this outstanding leadership team, and with our wonderful managers and crew members in the restaurants, we took on things beyond our control to find ways not only to survive but thrive. We came through Covid having learned a great deal about our business, our market, and what we're capable of. We also learned, via the ultimate stress test, that we had been on the right track all along: we had built a business that could come through hard times, and we had built it with the best people out there. Jim, Jeremy, and Lynne: I want to personally thank you here in my book for your commitment and hard work. Thanks to you, we not only survived the pandemic and kept our entire workforce working but we continued to grow our business. Considering so many businesses, especially restaurants, that suffered shattering losses or bankruptcy and closure during the pandemic, yours is a spectacular, singular achievement.

Another thing that I want to put out there: we felt great confidence in the administration from the federal level down. We'd never been through anything like this, but neither had they. It's a great feeling to see the men and women you've entrusted with the task of leadership, individuals such as President Donald J. Trump and New Hampshire Governor Chris Sununu, make wise decisions that strike the difficult balance between protecting our individual liberties and calling for sacrifice for the greater good of the state and the nation.

We've come through the other side. I'll never forget the experience, and I'll always appreciate these colleagues, customers, leaders, and friends who made it possible.

WONDERFUL (2022 AND BEYOND)

When I started school in America, I was afraid of being different, of dressing oddly, of not being able to speak English. Those obstacles were terrifying, but when I realized I could take them on, it gave me confidence. Overcoming them gave me satisfaction. This also made me hungry for more – more challenges to meet and more success from figuring them out. I loved that sense of independence. I still do. Add to that the love of my mother, the lessons from my father, and later, the joy of my wife and family and the satisfaction of my career with McDonald's – my approach to life was set. I was on a path to wonderful days, wonderful people, and wonderful experiences.

* * *

It's funny how you latch onto things.

Before she became my wife, I remember going on a date with Denise and bragging that someday I would have a house with a horseshoe driveway. No doubt I was trying to impress her with her suitor's ambition and architectural savoir faire.

I must have seen a house with a horseshow driveway and decided it was what a successful person might have – so this was my way of telling her that I intended to make something of myself. A house with a horseshoe driveway: that's how the teenage version of me measured the good life. I may have even seen it as the finish line.

Now I really do have a house with a horseshoe driveway, though I didn't mark its acquisition with the fanfare I envisioned back then. I appreciate what I have acquired over the years. But now that I'm in my 70s, I appreciate far more that I have had a wonderful life, a life allowed me by the grace of God. I take joy in having family, friends, and colleagues. I take satisfaction from having earned the success I dreamed of and having enjoyed the experience of getting here.

I always figured that if you worked hard, you could at least get the basics. You could have a roof over your head, keep a car in your garage or maybe two, accumulate a little money to not worry as much about every paycheck, build up the community for yourself and others, and go to sleep at night with a measure of security and satisfaction. With a little more effort and good luck here and there, even more, might be possible.

I dreamed of success, but I never thought I would reach the kind of success I have found.

To have a nice home – better than a nice home, actually – to keep a place at the Cape, to be able to whisk away my family on private planes, to have had enough to indulge in buying a car with the same nameplate as James Bond's... I never counted on any of that. When I was a younger man, I thought that if I worked very hard I might be able to snag an Oldsmobile Toronado, the one with a Rocket V8 under the hood and a slot-machine speedometer – the one they stopped making before I even turned 20.

My life today, and the life I share with my family, is a dream come true. I'm a blessed individual, I truly am.

* * *

So, why do I keep working?

I like the things I've accumulated, but far more than that I like the journey.

Strike that. I *love* the journey. Loved it way back when, and love it just as much today.

There's not much I enjoy more than the business of doing business. I appreciate the camaraderie of the people I work with. I get a thrill from competing with smart, honest entrepreneurs, because having that drive in common outweighs anything on which we might differ. I take satisfaction in creating opportunities for other people. I like improving my community and seeing how the results can enhance the lives of others. I take pleasure in running a company that drives economic progress and innovation. I'm proud to be an immigrant who helps other immigrants. I'm equally proud to spread the gospel of the opportunity that is the American way. I have fun being in the restaurant business. I like setting an example with the things I think I do well. And when I see a satisfied customer, I get a feeling that only comes from a job done right.

Counting your possessions is the wrong way to figure out who's made a life that matters. I like what I've accumulated. Who wouldn't? But I love far more what I've experienced and the connections with people I've made part of my life, and those who have made me a part of theirs.

On it goes. Not long before we sent this book to the printer, we purchased an additional 5 McDonald's restaurants in northern Maine from Heidi Abbotoni and her family. She was ready to retire, and we're always open to the right opportunity for growth. Not only did we acquire the restaurants, but we also were able to offer every member of Heidi's management and crew continued employment. As Ray Kroc always said, "Stay green and growing." We still are 66 restaurants and counting.

What else can I say? Every day is a lot of fun. Every moment is a joy.

It's been a wonderful life so far. I wonder what's next?

PART II: Rules for Success

INTRODUCTION

WHAT WORKED FOR ME...

I love success stories.

Whenever anyone tells me how they discovered their goals and what they did to achieve them, I always learn something.

Much of what I know about business and entrepreneurism has come from the hours I've spent with successful friends and colleagues – and, occasionally, strangers. Sometimes we're in professional settings and sometimes just socializing. It's good to be open to learning things wherever they come from.

That's what this part of my book is about.

Anyone successful in business borrows what works from other people. After you use those ideas for a while, you find that you've molded them to your situation and made them your own. I have had the benefit of knowing dozens of very successful people whose insights have influenced my career. I can't name every one of them, of course, yet everyone I've met in over a half-century in business has given me something I've made use of. Some folks, when we met, were already far into their career and success – far ahead of me at the time! – and were kind enough to share their secrets. Others were in more or less the same position as I was, and we learned from each other as we figured out the same problems. Even those folks who are just starting out could often show me things that turned out to be useful. But no matter where we were in our careers when we met, time made us both colleagues and friends.

There was Mr. McCoy, of course, who believed in me and gave me my first opportunity to succeed, along with his partner, Mr. Colley. (As I write this, I'm in my 70s yet I will always think of them as "Mister," never by their first names. Call it habit, call it respect.) I think of my friend and early supporter Lee Guercio, who was so exceptionally helpful when I opened the first restaurant I owned, even though he barely knew me. I think of my friend and fellow entrepreneur, Jordan Zimmerman, who built an advertising empire in much the same way I built my business. He introduced me to the gentleman who helped me assemble my experiences into the book you're reading now. There's my friend Franco Graceffa, a restaurateur like me who shares the belief that success comes from truly connecting with people and making them feel welcome and wanted.

So, yes, I love success stories, whether personal or professional. Here are some of mine.

FOR YOUR CAREER

BE WHERE YOU ARE NEEDED

Be there when you're needed. It may be for family. It may be for work. It may be for friends. But if you've made a commitment, honor it, and place no priority before it. When someone needs you, present yourself accordingly. Show up.

Over a hundred years ago, the great New England poet Robert Frost wrote a beautiful piece titled, "Death of the Hired Man." In it. he offered the line, "Home is the place where, when you have to go there, they have to take you in."

I've found that we're all "home" to somebody. The person they can come to, the one who will never turn them down in a time of need. You know who I'm talking about: your spouse, your child, your friend from way back.

But there's one other thing. Besides those folks, there are other people who feel that way about you, and you don't know who they are.

So, not only should you be where you're needed but you should be present and of service wherever you are.

Do it for them, but also do it for you.

BE GOOD TO YOUR CUSTOMERS

Whenever I think about my business, why we've been successful, and what really matters, I always end up back at customer satisfaction. It really is that simple: it's at the heart of my philosophy of business, and it's easy to understand.

It's not just good food at good prices. It's the whole experience, or what my son Sal calls "the environment."

We build the McDonald's environment for our customers toward that expectation. In the beginning, it was something we stressed when someone joined our team. These days, we still do that, but we also do it formally, as part of training. Take care of the customers' experience, and every good thing follows.

I have a good friend who shares my attitude. His name is Franco Graceffa, and he owns a beloved Italian restaurant on Hanover Street in Boston's famous North End. Every day, he delivers a perfect demonstration of customer service – real hospitality. Like so many people in our own organization, Franco's route to success included a lot of fascinating moments whose lessons would serve him well throughout life.

Franco was born in Sicily, near Sciacca, and he didn't start out in the restaurant business. The closest he came in his youth was spending time in his mother's kitchen, but that sparked his interest. As a young man, he earned a degree in electrical engineering, then served in the Italian army. After he was discharged, he came to visit his sister in America, where he fell in love with this country. In 1974, he came here permanently and soon started his own successful business. Eventually, he fell in love with a wonderful woman, then fulfilled his dream by opening Dolce Vita Ristorante, which is Italian for "sweet life."

When I talk to our people about hospitality, I always tell them about Franco. Hospitality starts with how you greet your customers, and you should do what's appropriate for the place you are. In our restaurants, that means a greeting and a smile, and showing real interest in the person in front of you. At Dolce Vita, Franco greets his customers as if they were already friends – and some of them are. Be prepared to receive a hug and a kiss (although COVID slowed that down considerably, at least if he didn't know you). What matters to Franco is what should matter to everyone in the restaurant business: warmth, friendliness, and making people feel welcome and wanted. If you're around late enough in the evening, he'll even serenade you! I don't think he'll mind if I tell you he's a great singer and, after a couple of glasses of wine, he'll sing along with the musician who might be playing in the restaurant. You might hear him favor the room with the "Love Theme from *The Godfather*," a classic from Tony Bennett, or even old Sicilian songs. It's always wonderful.

Franco creates a wonderful environment because he knows that as magnificent as the food and service are, people are touched by something more, something that gives them an experience. You must put people in an environment that makes the whole thing worthwhile – otherwise, they won't be coming back.

It's easy to believe that once you have a quality good or service, you've taken care of everything. But you don't.

The experience of being in the restaurant and experiencing the hospitality of the people who work there is the biggest basic of all. Everybody who works there has to keep this in mind.

When I was thinking about how to explain this aspect of customer satisfaction and what it has meant to my success, it occurred to me that some people might read about Franco's restaurant and the atmosphere there versus a McDonald's restaurant and the atmosphere there and conclude that we're talking about apples and oranges.

Man, oh, man – if that's what you think, you've made a terrible mistake. In the middle of all that, I said a key thing: the way you conduct yourself in terms of hospitality depends on the situation. A hug and a handshake make sense for a Saturday-night dinner in an intimate restaurant, while a smile and a kind word make sense at a busy lunchtime in a McDonald's in Concord, New Hampshire.

But they're both a demonstration of hospitality, caring about the customer, and creating the appropriate environment for your customer.

It all comes down to hospitality. Do what makes people comfortable and welcome. Keep customer satisfaction number one.

BE GOOD TO YOUR EMPLOYEES

Not long ago, on a weekend-drive home, I stopped by the Leominster, Massachusetts, restaurant. The manager saw me and came over immediately.

"Pete," he said, "something's come up. My wife is outside and I really have to go with her."

That might not have been a problem, and certainly not something that concerned me, except that on this day the crew was already shorthanded – and no one else was around.

The manager didn't have to say what he was really asking: he wanted me, not just his boss but the fellow who owns the company, to cover for him.

If he left and someone didn't take his place, the restaurant would be not only shorthanded but also unable to serve customers in the way we require.

I told him that I understood his predicament and that I would hang around to help so he could go. My wife was expecting me, so I called her to explain that I would be out until closing time.

Did I have to cover for this employee? No. I could have told him he wasn't allowed to go, and I could have gone home to dinner on a lovely Saturday afternoon in New England.

But just as I ask my employees to go the extra mile, I need to be ready to do it myself.

This gentleman had been with me a long time, starting years before as a crew member. He was a faithful associate who was in a bind, I could help, and I wanted him to know I was grateful for his service. But I was just as grateful for the responsibility he had shown. He wasn't making a frivolous request. He had a serious, personal reason that called him away. Until I walked in, it had not occurred to him to do anything but stay at his job.

In other words, he was doing the responsible thing even though he could have slipped out and gotten away with it.

When your people do the responsible thing when no one's watching, it is incumbent on management to do the kind thing in response. These kinds of interactions build trust, reliability, and collegiality, and those are the foundations of a successful business.

HELP YOUR EMPLOYEES SUCCEED

From the early days when I managed the restaurant in Leominster through today, we make it a priority to create opportunities for our employees. It makes me happy to see people succeed, especially when they're reaching for their dreams. If they see that you're helping them pursue their ambitions, they're going to do good work, and the benefit accrues to both of you. It's as simple as that.

If somebody takes what they've learned from us and moves on to a new career? We're happy with that, too. They'll carry with them their positive attitude, their commitment to courtesy, and their belief in the importance of providing a quality product and first-rate service. Spreading some good to the world – that's a win.

Of course that doesn't mean I want people to join us and move on. I always hope that they'll stay, take on more responsibility, and move up in our organization. But whether they stay with us or move on, I want the best for them, and so does everyone else in our management.

If we hire them in the first place, it's because we see something in them and think it's a good match. I'm confident in their character and commitment because of our hiring process. It's more than matching skills with job requirements. We consider what the person who fills a given position will be doing in relation to the attitude and aptitude we see in them. The way they approach an opportunity tells you a lot of what you need to know. A good leader recognizes these capacities often before the person.

Help your employees succeed, first by matching them well to the work, then by encouraging their dreams and ambitions. Everybody wins.

GET ALONG WITH PEOPLE, EVEN IF THEY DON'T GET ALONG WITH YOU

It was a Sunday night. The restaurant I was visiting had been a little shorthanded lately, so I had stepped in myself, as much to help as to get some firsthand experience with a young manager we had been bringing along. We thought he might do well with an opportunity to take on more responsibility.

After business slowed for the evening, I sat down with this manager to discuss a few things: what was going well, what could be done a little better, and what he thought we could offer to make his job easier and his work more effective. His wife joined us. She worked there as well as an hourly employee. I'd already spent time with the two of them the week before, so I felt we had some rapport. I began our conversation with that.

"As I was saying last week when I took you out to dinner—"

"You didn't take us for dinner," said the manager's wife. "The company did." Wow, did she take me by surprise! She was right, I hadn't picked up the tab. The company had.

But that wasn't the point. With an attitude like that, it was clear she didn't understand the point of the conversation – or the possibilities she was kicking away.

It was an indication of poor judgment, and not just hers. Her husband was the real focus of the conversation, and this meeting had suddenly gone from a casual engagement to a test. This young manager needed to defuse a delicate situation. It wasn't the offending comment that mattered. He's not the one who made it.

No, what mattered was whether he could recognize what had happened and defuse the situation. Yet he didn't backpedal, dispute, or apologize. He didn't even try to change the subject. He just sat there, his silence suggesting that he didn't see anything wrong with what he had just heard and, apparently, endorsed.

You often learn about someone's character by what they say and do, but you can learn just as much from what they don't say. This young man didn't seem to know how to get along with other people, or how important that skill is. The success or failure of someone managing or supervising a McDonald's restaurant depends in large part on their ability to get along with other people.

You don't have to flatter folks. You don't have to say things you don't mean. But you do need to be able to recognize communication gone wrong and a wrench unnecessarily tossed toward a relationship. Success demands getting along with people.

SIDEBAR: WHAT I LEARNED FROM MCDONALD'S FOUNDER RAY KROC

Most of the times I met Ray Kroc were before I was an owner-operator before there was a Napoli Group. I would be in an audience and Mr. Kroc would be giving a talk from a stage or the front of a room. He was at once dynamic and down to earth. When he spoke, he used no notes. In some ways, it would sound as if he was talking off the top of his head. I recall one day he stepped to the mic and shouted, *What do you guys do for us?*

We're area supervisors! we shouted back.

Then it would be clear that he wasn't making it up as he went along. He knew his company so well that he could simply tell us from experience things that would help us do our jobs better, and he could keep it up for ten minutes or two hours. He'd done all the jobs. He'd *created* all the jobs.

If I were an area supervisor, he'd say, *this is how I would do my job,* then he would proceed to tell us. He never took the easy way out, talking about his philosophy of business or regaling us with stories that might have been fun to hear but wouldn't be about the topic at hand. No, Mr. Kroc would walk us through the job as he believed – as he knew – it ought to be done. In the case of an area supervisor, I still remember what he said. He started at the very beginning, telling us about pulling up at the restaurant, then walking around to make sure there was no litter and picking up anything he found, securing the parking lot, then coming inside to make sure the restaurant itself is spotless, especially the restrooms, and then come in and evaluate every product to make sure it met the standards.

That's what you have to do, he'd say, and the way he presented it made you want to go back and do your job that much better. He was a very inspiring gentleman.

So when Mr. Kroc had something to say, it was worth listening to.

Mr. Kroc, whom I did meet in person first in Toronto, Canada, and a few times after, built his restaurants on systems and procedures that ensure consistency in quality, taste, and overall experience. It started with the raw products, and he did a great job with that, as with everything. He insisted on buying the best ingredients, and he also demanded the best equipment.

Mr. Kroc always insisted on quality control. He would have inspectors come in and tell you what you did well and what you needed to do better. I'm a little prejudiced, of course, but I think McDonald's is the best in the industry at keeping quality high. The organization is what it is today because of our founder, Ray Kroc.

KNOW EVERY JOB BECAUSE NONE IS BENEATH YOU

When I started as a crew member, I learned to do all the jobs in the restaurant. When we needed someone to fill in, I could do so at the drop of a hat. So could our other employees. It was a condition of employment.

This had a benefit I discovered not long after. When I became a manager, I had a profound appreciation for what my employees were doing day in and day out. If I hadn't done all their jobs, I probably would have greatly underestimated how important each role is to the success of the operation.

Whatever business you're in, make it a priority to have practical knowledge of as many jobs around you as you can. If you can learn to do them, even better.

If you move up into management, you will supervise every job in the organization. You can't manage very well if you don't understand every job, and a manager understands every job best by being able to do every job. This also makes you a useful participant when a staffing problem arises.

A manager's ability to fill in anywhere he or she is needed is a powerful secret weapon. If a role in the restaurant has to go unfilled for even an hour, the customers feel the effect. The "crunch" among your staff means that there is less focus on creating a welcoming environment for guests and less attention to maintaining the high quality of what you're preparing.

Great managers and useful executives do not show up in the morning just to stay behind a desk. They show up ready to play, if and when needed.

Everybody in our office, including Sal and myself as owners, is always ready to get our hands dirty, and we often do. You can't decide that you're too important to pick up a broom, take an order, or wipe down a table. A lot of security and value flows from having a manager-as-backup who is always good to go.

This was a priority when I first joined under Mr. McCoy and Mr. Colley, and I'm proud to say that it remains a priority today.

DON'T FIGHT CHANGE: WELCOME IT

I have seen the McDonald's business go from serving customers at the front counter with no inside seating, no drive-thru, and no breakfast service, to having all that plus delivery, mobile ordering, and electronic payment. By the time you read this, we'll no doubt have even more ways to serve our customers and support our employees.

Life moves pretty fast, and change isn't always easy, but the wise play is to treat change as a friend. Everything I listed in that first paragraph? There were more than a few people who, when they first heard about them, said, "That's no good. Now we're going to have to deal with people ordering from their cars!"

Of course, anyone who didn't adapt to the concept of the drive-thru has long been left behind. Those who made the switch early built up their businesses in ways they never imagined.

Welcome the change that comes your way. By the way, on this matter, you don't have a choice. If you can't adapt, I don't care what industry you're in, you will not be successful.

Finally, be prepared for change by creating space for it. Prune things that aren't working to make room for new things that might – that's how you grow. Even if you don't know what's coming, and usually you don't, you must be prepared. Opportunity never comes without change. Change is a friend.

RESTING ON YOUR ACHIEVEMENTS IS GOING BACKWARD: KEEP GROWING

If you rest on your laurels thinking that you can just hold your position in the market by holding your position in the market, you're wrong.

To keep thriving, you have to keep moving. In business, that means expanding your reach.

Businesses are either growing or shrinking. There is no "holding steady." That's because there's always competition, always a changing marketplace, always the evolving expectations of your customers, and always something that will require you to adjust the way you do business. To consolidate your gains, aim to do more than consolidate. Set your sights on continuing to expand your reach.

Around the time I started writing this book, the Napoli Group purchased a cluster of five McDonald's restaurants near the Canadian border. It was an opportunity for growth, and we took it. Simply remaining in place is not a business strategy for success but for failure. We know that the only way to stay successful is to expand.

But growth for its own sake isn't smart, either.

Every year, several McDonald's owners reach out to us to ask if we're interested in buying their restaurants. Most of the time we say no.

Growth that builds success means we don't just take every deal that comes along, even when the price seems right. Random growth isn't productive growth. In the case of our most recent purchase, we did due diligence, as we always do. We examined the restaurants as physical and financial entities, plus we considered all the elements that go into making a successful restaurant. Finally, we considered how such an acquisition would advance our own goals.

We recently concluded a purchase in northern Maine. To demonstrate how we approach such decisions, I'll walk you through this one.

First, these restaurants are in the right location for us, meaning they are near other restaurants we own, which makes it reasonable for us to support them. In addition, this group naturally expands the market we are already in.

Second, these restaurants have been well managed for many years, they have an established place in the community, they come with no marketing issues to overcome, and they have strong financials, which means that we don't have to do any administrative or financial "clean up." In other words, we're not taking on hidden expenses as part of this growth.

Finally, these restaurants have been modernized in the last ten years, meaning they were torn down and rebuilt. In terms of the physical plant, our future reinvestment will be minimal. With a new restaurant costing millions of dollars, that's important.

The answer is clear: this is an opportunity for growth and

expansion that aligns with the way we do business and will contribute to our continued profitability and success. This is a purchase we decided to make.

We weren't the only ones who had thought about what would make this a wise acquisition. The couple who owned these McDonald's had started thinking about this sale years before. They had taken over the restaurants from their family. In fact, the wife had grown up in the business. Their restaurants are in superb financial condition and carry no debt. This husband and wife, in their mid-50s, had long had the goal of retiring young, so they planned, anticipating what a buyer would be looking for – hence the sound financial picture and the new physical plants. They intended to sell their five restaurants so they could live comfortably for the rest of their lives, using the proceeds of the sale to generate investment income. As a result of all this care on their end, they anticipated the investigation that would come from our end, prepared for it, and passed it with flying colors. You might say it was an offer we couldn't refuse!

They had taken good care of the business so it would be attractive to a buyer. They knew better than to run things haphazardly and then hope for the best.

Since I know that growth is a requirement for continued success, we're always open to a growth opportunity, as long as it fits into our plans and our organization.

When restaurants are poised for growth, we're interested.

When restaurants have the right long-term operating costs, we're interested.

When we can make back our investment and run the restaurants successfully, we're interested.

Finally – and frankly – we also ask ourselves how we feel about it overall. Call it a gut check.

When you've been at this as long as we have, you know that the numbers on the page don't tell the whole story. Intuition matters. Sometimes that nagging feeling you get when you're considering a deal is telling you something valuable. Sometimes it's telling you that there's something you're not considering – and to be careful. Other times, it's telling you that even if everything doesn't quite add up on the spreadsheet, this is a great opportunity that you shouldn't miss.

Growth is a vital element of success. When you attempt to grow, do it carefully and thoughtfully to ensure it's the right kind of growth.

NEVER LOWER YOUR STANDARDS

In the late 1980s, the McDonald's corporation experimented with locations in shopping malls and other high-traffic locations that were part of larger retail centers. We followed their lead and put quite a few of our restaurants in local Walmart stores. But in our part of the country, the project didn't work. The volume of customers wasn't sufficient to support our expenses, especially the cost of labor.

In simple terms, we didn't have enough sales to cover expenses.

Your first thought might be that we could have just staffed fewer people or paid everybody a little less. But in the long run, saving money that way would have cost more.

The way McDonald's operates, we hire highly qualified, well-trained management teams. Those do not come cheap. To cut corners on those expenses would have resulted in inferior products and inferior service.

You know how I feel about that.

If you can't run a restaurant the way it ought to be run, it first becomes a distraction and then a problem. From that, the problems would have fallen like dominoes. In this case, that sub-standard performance would have been a stain on our reputation, and when you damage your reputation, you're damaging a lot more than the restaurants that caused the problem in the first place. You're doing damage to the brand.

When the brand is damaged, you've come full circle: you've damaged your ability to sustain your good reputation. If you lose your reputation, you lose your ability to drive traffic. That is a direct path to the end of the line, leaving you with a bunch of low-traffic restaurants that can't be sustained – all because you let your standards slip in the first low-traffic restaurant.

So understaffing for the sake of staying open? No way. When the choice is to lower your standards or shut it down, I shut it down. I did it then, and I'd do it today.

If you think shuttering a business is costly, wait until you see the price of keeping an inferior operation on the books.

Never lower your standards.

RUN THE BUSINESS LIKE YOU OWN IT

This one I owe to my son, Sal. It's one of his guiding principles, though I like to think he learned it from watching his dad.

I have always conducted myself as if I owned the restaurant where I worked, even when I didn't. It's what I did as a crew member, and it's what I did as a manager, so I've been doing this long before I owned any restaurants.

No matter where you are in the hierarchy of the organization, there is no better way than to keep your actions in line with the best interests of the company. That's good for your job and your career in the long term. There are lots of ways to act on this advice, but I'll share five of the best for managers:

- Hire the best people
- Provide first-class training
- Motivate your people well
- Ensure a great work environment for everyone
- Provide compensation that is higher than the industry standard

Run it like you own it: this is a key principle that has driven my success. It may be the most important thing I know. I kept this in mind as a manager working for Mr. McCoy. The result? When I assumed ownership of my restaurants, this principle was already fixed in my head. That meant that the switchover from the employee to the owner was smooth as glass because I didn't have to suddenly change my mindset. For nearly two decades, I had focused on how my day-to-day decisions affected the big picture.

I always made decisions as if it were my name, my reputation, and my business on the line. Not only did this provide a constant motivation to make the best choices in the decisions before me, but it was also the right thing to do. Mr. McCoy and the Colley/McCoy Company had put their trust in me, and I was determined to prove to them that they had made a wise decision.

Sal calls this "owning the environment," and I think that keeping this phrase in mind is an excellent way to convert this attitude into action. Think about the difference between how you treat something that belongs to you versus how you treat something that's just given to you for a time, something disposable, something that will pass through your hands without anyone ever knowing you had any influence. Of course, you'll care less, and it will come through in the way you treat that thing.

So own the environment, even if it's only in your mind.

If you see someone not performing their duties quite as effectively, efficiently, or as good as you need it to be, offer to help. Just as managers need to be comfortable doing the work of the crew members, managers should empower crew members to help each other, encourage each other, and offer insights and instruction because it can benefit everyone.

We care most about the things that belong to us. It turns out that even pretending we own something will motivate us toward greater excellence. It puts us in the mindset that raises quality for everyone.

YOU AREN'T THE BEST FIT FOR EVERYTHING, SO DELEGATE

As I was working on this passage, I was supposed to have a call with the individual who is helping me assemble this material. I went to our conference room to wait for our video meeting to begin. While I waited, I continued making my notes for our conversation. But when the meeting began, we had a technology problem: I couldn't hear the fellow on the other end! I tinkered with the computer myself but with no luck. In a moment, it occurred to me to follow my own advice: delegate. I'm no good with technology. What was I doing? I called for someone else to come in and have a look at the system – someone who knows the system. She immediately came in and began troubleshooting.

Meanwhile, I returned to preparing my notes for the conversation to come.

I had nothing to contribute in terms of trying to help with tech. I'd be wasting my time and slowing down my on-site expert. So, I made good use of my time by doing what I could do, which at that moment was to further prepare for the meeting. I called in someone who could do what they did best: troubleshoot the videoconference system.

In a few minutes, the support person got the system up and running again. Meanwhile, I used my time to prepare further for my conversation. The result was a more efficient use of everyone's time, more satisfaction in the work that was done, and ultimately a book, the one you're reading right now. We got there faster because I delegated instead of rising to the bait so many people fall for – trying to do everything yourself.

Even when you can do it all, that's not the best move. I could pitch in over at the human resources department and pick up the slack in accounting if I need to – remember what I wrote about being able to do every job? But in this situation, that wasn't a constructive use of my skills and time. A wise manager delegates – not to avoid work, of course, but to get all work done more efficiently and professionally.

FOR YOURSELF

DON'T BE DISTRACTED

There are lots of reasons for a leader's success, but one of the most important is he or she deals with what's in front of them and rejects distraction. It doesn't matter if the other thing in front of you is a problem or an opportunity. In the moment, stick with your knitting. Do what's in front of you. Don't bail on one thing to suddenly take up another.

This is easier said than done, of course. The temptation is strong. That's why you must make a conscious choice to focus on the task at hand before you even begin. Tell yourself what you're going to do – and what you're not going to do. It may even help to say it out loud! You have to do this because every few minutes a new distraction can arise, and you're going to feel a strong pull to take your eyes off the job of the moment to pursue it.

The most attractive temptation in life is the opportunity for something to take us out of the moment and potentially reward us with quick success. As human beings, we love the feeling of completing something, so the opportunity to jump into something new and "fix it" is going to draw us. Practice resisting and plan your defense.

Before I begin some task, I turn off my phone, shut off my email, and clear the calendar so I'm not dealing with other obligations during the time I've set aside for working on a particular thing.

I tell my young managers to be careful of that cell phone. If you're the boss, make sure you're the boss of not just the people but also of that pocket-sized machine. That phone can easily become a ball and chain – or, worse, a leash that can yank you away from important work and into distraction after distraction at any moment.

In the long run, when you stick with the job that's in front of you until it's done, you're going to get more done, find more satisfaction, and enjoy superior outcomes.

In the restaurant business, I've had plenty of chances to put this into practice. Consider those times when you're in the middle of a couple of busy hours, maybe the lunch rush. You can't step away from your work as a manager to take a phone call because that takes you out of the role that is vital in the moment, whether it's being a coach or captain, or even filling in for someone on the crew or picking up the slack when things are extra tight. In that moment – in every moment – you have a role to play, and failing to play your role affects the entire team and their effectiveness.

This is important for your personal life, too. Rejecting distraction enhances your enjoyment of the time you make your own and makes it clear to the people around you that they are your first priority. Think of how you feel when you're talking with someone and they interrupt your conversation to take a call or even to do something else. You feel slighted, and you may think less of them. You don't want it done to you, so don't do it to other people.

The other day my wife and I were at lunch with one of our grandchildren, Jake. He had just graduated from junior high so we took him to one of his favorite places to eat. As we were wrapping up, my wife received a message from a decorator who was working on our house. She wanted us to select a piece of furniture based on some samples he sent. It was a trivial decision, something we could do in only a moment. It would have taken no time at all.

"Let's table it," I said. "We'll deal with this in the morning over coffee." With that, we continued, not having missed a second of our lovely outing with our handsome and brilliant grandson on the occasion of his graduation. Could we have replied to the decorator right then and there, and quickly? Of course! But that wasn't where our focus belonged. Life is short. Grandchildren are precious. That decorator will be there tomorrow. As for me, I'll take every second of the best part of life – and I want Jake to know who matters most to us. It's one thing to tell somebody they matter. It's something much better for them to see your priorities in action.

For the first 40 years of my career – come to think of it, that's most of it! – I would never bring my briefcase into the house. When the cell phone came on the scene, I would not bring that into the house, either. When you work 60, 70, or even more hours a week, you need some disconnect from work and to pay attention to the people at home. No distractions.

The good news is that doing what's in front of you is a habit you can develop fast. I suggest you practice constantly. I do. At the end of each day, you can look back and see how well you did.

The first time is the hardest. The second's a little easier. But it's easier every time from there on out. That's how you improve, and the results will be dramatic.

The more you apply this to every part of your life, not just work, the most satisfying every part of your life will be.

The sooner you begin, the better.

DON'T FOCUS ON THE PROBLEM: FOCUS ON FIXING IT

Once I've encountered a difficult situation, I do not spend time jawboning about how much pain it might be causing. When something is a problem, it's a problem. Carrying on about it doesn't do a thing to fix it.

So, don't focus on the problem. Turn your attention to finding solutions. Don't waste a second indulging your worries.

It's easier said than done, of course. I can get upset over little things, but I try to remember that getting upset is a waste of everyone's time. Usually, I can get back on track pretty quickly.

It's a simple truth, but it carries a lot of power: recounting your troubles doesn't fix your troubles.

You know what fixes your troubles? Fixing your troubles.

TREAT SUCCESS LIKE A JOURNEY, NOT A DESTINATION

I'm proud when people compliment me by saying that I have "reached" success. I know what they mean, and I appreciate the thought, but the way they put it isn't quite what happened to me. It's true enough that success takes a lifetime, but if you're doing it the right way, the best way, the experience itself has been an experience in success.

As the old saying goes, success is not a destination but a journey.

No one wakes up to find success knocking at the door. Opportunity? Sure, sometimes. But to think of success as a destination is to misunderstand what success is all about.

Success is satisfaction in what you're doing.

Success is giving back to your community, taking care of your family, showing kindness to your friends, and presenting a generous spirit toward all. It's thinking hard about why we're here and finding purpose in life. Is it about joy? Not exactly. Happiness for its own sake doesn't yield a life well lived. It doesn't even produce a happy life – which is ironic. For life to be fulfilling, it needs a purpose.

I have found over the years that the pursuit of success – not the arrival at some destination measured in dollars and cents, but the pursuit of doing good and right things – *that* is success.

When you choose to live that way, you are enjoying success all along the way.

Success is a journey, not a destination.

The satisfaction of improving oneself spins off benefits for everyone around you, but it brings an especially good feeling to you when you wake up in the morning. I want to get better at what I do every day. Hopefully, I will be better at all this tomorrow than I am today. Even a little improvement is a good thing. It doesn't have to be huge. Moving forward, moving toward a goal, and doing it with honor and integrity and wisdom and grace – that's what matters. That's the definition of success. It's a road I love to travel.

SIDEBAR:
A CONVERSATION WITH THE GOVERNOR

As I prepared this book, I spoke with a lot of old friends. Some offered a reminiscence or two. Others reminded me of times we shared that I had almost forgotten.

This one's a little different.

As we were finishing this book, I sat down with my friend, Governor of New Hampshire, Chris Sununu. His father, John Sununu, was also a New Hampshire governor, as well as White House chief of staff under President George H. W. Bush – quite an accomplished family. Governor Sununu and I sat down for a chat – because I like him, and he likes me, and because we share many of the same values, especially when it comes to community, commitment, and the obligation to give back to the places we come from. This is a bit of our conversation.

You know how it is when friends talk. There's a lot of back and forth and more than a little jumping in on each other and laughing. With that in mind, I've boiled down our chat to a summary. It's not a word-for-word transcript, not at all, but it gives you the gist of what we said that day, and I wanted to share it here with you.

Governor Sununu is a great man. I'm lucky to know him, and I'm sure you'll enjoy our engagement almost – *almost* – as much as we did.

Gov. Chris Sununu of New Hampshire: Peter, my relationship with you goes back to my godfather, Rick McCoy, who was a great friend of my dad's. In 1969, my folks moved to the same neighborhood as Mr. McCoy, and he and my father became fast friends. When my father was elected governor in 1982, one of his first acts was serving McDonald's to every state employee in the building. He called up Rick's restaurant and ordered something like a thousand Egg McMuffins and brought them into the Statehouse!

A few years before I became governor myself, I met Peter.

When Rick McCoy got out of the business and Peter purchased his stores, he did more than just keep doing business. What Peter, Sal, and the Napoli family have always done is to create an atmosphere where you walk into one of the largest food franchises in the country but you feel like you're in something local. You're not just the next person in line. You're someone who matters. You might even be someone they know.

I know that sounds a little cliché, but it's true. When I grew up in Salem, I knew everybody behind the counter.

That's Peter Napoli's model, and it is not something anyone can take for granted because it is not easy. He has done a phenomenal thing. Not only is it a great way to do business, but it's also a reflection of how we live here in New Hampshire. We are the *Live Free or Die* state, and we are all about local control. We're not about big governments and big systems and big this and big that. To be successful, even when big things come into our state, they have to keep it local and real. Every community is different. Every customer is different. That has to be reflected in how you do business. If you treat people like that, it can be a real model for success.

Let me give you an example from outside the walls of Peter's McDonald's. Before I became governor, I ran the Waterville Valley Ski Resort. For decades, the resort has hosted the Special Olympics, and Peter has long been a part of that – but not in the way you might think. Peter's family gave a big check, but that was just the beginning. Peter and the whole Napoli family and organization get involved from doing the work on the ground of delivering meals to stepping up, year after year, as a hands-on partner at every level. We're grateful for everyone who contributes, but there's a special place in our hearts for those friends and neighbors who step up in this way.

Peter: As an entrepreneur in the state of New Hampshire, I look at it as our obligation to help people. Special Olympians deserve our support. When we can do things to make their quality of life a little better, you can bet we'll be there. I'll give a big measure of credit to Mr. McCoy. He was an inspiration to me, of course. Your godfather was a great teacher on how to run a good restaurant and how to be a good neighbor, but underneath all of that was always the importance of keeping the community at the center of whatever you do.

Sununu: As you know, I have teenagers plus one small one at home. Our daughter is working just now as a hostess at a restaurant in Exeter. When we drive past McDonald's, she tells me what she's hearing about incentive programs and scholarship opportunities for teens like her working at Peter's restaurants – plus you can see it on the signs in the windows! The other day, she told me that while she likes where she works just fine, she is beginning to wonder if she's missing out on a lot of things that Peter Napoli provides for young people like her looking toward work, careers, and further education. "I like where I am, but maybe I made the wrong decision," she said.

I know what she means because I know that what Peter's done over the years for young people goes so deep that if I filled her in, she might quit her current job and apply at Peter's restaurant right away. Peter has put a lot of kids through school, given them opportunities they wouldn't otherwise have, and given them a pathway into working for a living and finding a career in whatever it is they love. This, in turn, is part of why people stay so loyal to Peter. He and the Napoli Group have invested so profoundly in them that they feel like part of a family, and they stay loyal – not just to him, but to the mission he's taken on himself for our communities.

Unemployment is very low just now across the country and here in New Hampshire, and we're proud of our part in making that a reality. But the downside for business operators is that it can be hard to find workers. You don't want to cut hours. You want to reward loyalty with loyalty. That's what Peter does – so he has built a measure of insulation for his business from this kind of challenge. He stays loyal to his people, they stay loyal to him, and the business grows, even as the contribution to the community continues and expands. He's been doing that for decades – literally decades.

That kind of commitment to opportunity over so many, many years is humbling as a citizen and eye-opening as a parent. As governor, I want to see this in this state. It's the right thing to do.

It builds generation after generation of young people who learn by doing and by example what they must do to be successful.

That's pretty awesome.

One more thing: I interact with Peter and his family on many fronts, but there's one where we work together more often than any other, and that's our shared respect for law enforcement. We believe in these men and women because what they do is indispensable. Respect for officers – you don't see that across this country right now, especially with things such as the Defund the Police movement, and so many businesses walking away from law enforcement. But one group standing strong with law enforcement has been and always will be Peter Napoli's McDonald's.

Peter: That's a compliment I'll take, Governor. It's true. We're committed to the law enforcement community and all the officers who protect us. We're going to keep writing checks to keep the resources behind it.

Sununu: One more time: Peter doesn't just write that check and move on. He and his family and his organization get involved personally. They're always there whether it's the Coffee with a Cop program, scholarships, or donations to nonprofit organizations within the law enforcement community. The effect is more powerful and more personal. It's certainly been long-lasting, too. We're not going to back away from that one iota. If anything, we're going to double down on it. While a few other folks in the country may walk away, we're going to double down.

As governor, I can tell you that it is so important to see that kind of commitment. We didn't have any of those issues you saw in other parts of the country in part because we have individuals like Peter making that commitment, translating their mission into action. They believe in their communities, and they know where the investments and the commitment have to maintain the foundation and infrastructure of a healthy community. Law enforcement and public safety: very often, that's where it all starts and stops with law enforcement. I've always just had an unbelievable admiration – don't blush, Peter…

Peter: Ha!

Sununu: I believe in what he's done and the commitments he's made through his business and his family. Cops can count on Peter because of the way he conducts business and lives his life. Cops don't stay around for the pay, trust me. They could get a lot more money doing something else. But they love what they do. They're committed to their communities. So, we owe it to them – and to ourselves – to recognize what they do and to support them at every turn.

Peter: Governor, thank you. I'm glad we're partners in our communities. I'm glad we're working for good things for the people who live and work here.

Sununu: You're one more reason New Hampshire's a great state.

DON'T CELEBRATE TOO MUCH

We love celebrating, and why shouldn't we? Celebrating victories is not only fun but also important. It recognizes achievement and lets people know that you appreciate them. But once the celebration is done, you can't keep hanging around after the party's over. You have to get back to the business at hand, which is delivering excellence.

Here's an example. We have modernized and rebuilt many McDonald's restaurants. When I say that we "rebuilt" them, what I mean is that we've torn down an old McDonald's and built a new one from scratch. Such a project comes with a lot of exciting, interesting, and challenging work. We have to make a lot of decisions in a short amount of time. Once the restaurant is complete and ready for a grand reopening, we like to celebrate, but we're careful about how we do that – rather, we're careful about how long we do that.

Having the new building in place is a mark that you've achieved a lot, so the temptation can be to rest on your laurels – but you can't. Getting to this point is the reason for a celebration, but you quickly have to get back to work because there's so much more to do, including training the team on the new setup, ensuring the cleanliness and sanitation systems for the rebuilt building, making plans for the grand opening itself, transferring all the legal and mechanical matters from the old building to the new one, and making preparations for the guests who will come help you mark the fresh beginning in this new facility. There's a place for celebration, and there's value in it. The promise of a celebration can be a great motivator, too. But the smart move is to celebrate and then go to the next thing. There will always be more reasons to celebrate down the road, but if you stay in celebration mode for too long, you won't reach those opportunities.

Have there been times when my team and I celebrated too much? For us, and most successful people, I think that's the wrong way to look at it. After you get through a big task and you celebrate success, it's not so much that the celebration goes on too long as you lose the impetus to return to the previous level of effort. In other words, you lose some steam.

The good news is that if you plan for it, you can avoid this problem. You don't have to celebrate less, but you do need to be mindful of the pitfalls of not getting back to work and of the potential "letdown" that comes after any success. The thrill of victory is fun to savor, but the job requires moving on to the next challenge. Successful people are always on the lookout for the next hill to climb. There's satisfaction in that. There's pleasure in that. And knowing this is a critical part of maintaining success – and personal satisfaction.

CHOOSE TO BE HAPPY

Whenever I speak to our employees, I try to spend some time encouraging them to look for a positive way of approaching any situation.

If you think back over your life, the things you remember most are the times you overcame some obstacle. The days when everything was normal and life came at you the way you expected… those memories fade away. What we remember are those moments when a problem came our way, and it was up to us to fix it. In short, we remember triumph over challenge.

That's why it's so important to approach every day with a positive attitude: the things we do that matter most are most successfully met when we decide up front that we are going to look for the happy, hopeful, or promising things, and cast aside the temptation to dwell on what might go wrong.

You can call it the power of positive thinking if you like – a lot of people do. I just think of it as one more form of the wise way to do things. When a problem comes along, I try to take it as an opportunity, not as a reason to be frustrated.

Which doesn't mean I'm going to overcome it the first time I take it on. Positive thinking also includes picking yourself up after you fail. Over the years, as a manager since 1971, there were times when I would go home and say, *Holy cow, what a day! I really got kicked around.* But the next morning, I would wake up with new ideas about how to deal with the problem from the day before, and I'd go in and try it. Most of the time, that did the trick. It's easy to get overwhelmed with difficult situations, but patience and tenacity, powered by a positive outlook, usually make the difference – and that's true whether it's a problem at work or something at home.

As I reflect on this idea, I'm thinking about how it's not anything you haven't heard before. For that reason alone, it might feel like something you can ignore. But just because this advice is common doesn't make it less valuable. The fact is that how you deal with difficulties will determine your degree of happiness and success.

Ask anybody what they want out of life, and they'll give you some version of the same answer: a good job, a family, money, success. But if you scratch the surface just beyond those answers, you'll realize that what we really want out of life is just to be happy.

Facing every challenge with a positive attitude is one of the most powerful ways to experience happiness throughout your life.

Happiness doesn't just happen to you. I have found in my more than 70 years on this earth that happiness is first and foremost one thing: a choice.

LISTEN AND LEARN

I don't have all the answers. No one person does. That's why it's important to listen.

If you hear something you can make use of, do so – wherever it comes from. Everyone's capable of a good idea, and by listening to a variety of people, you'll hear things you would never have thought of yourself.

One of the reasons I've written this book is that I've figured out a few things over the years that are useful for building and maintaining success. I decided that if I put them all together in one place, my children's children and their children might find it a little easier to build successful lives of their own. I like to think of my book as an opportunity for people to put to use what they hear – or, in this case, read.

I got things right, and I got things wrong, hopefully more of the former than the latter. I want to get as much mileage out of the experience as possible. All this worked for me, and I believe it'll work for anyone who tries it, and I especially want success for my family whom I love so much.

There's a reason you have only one mouth but two ears. We should all listen more.

WHEN YOU'RE IN THE RIGHT, DON'T BACK DOWN

If you have a vision – a sense of direction on how to make your business better – stick to it. Refuse to be pulled in another direction. Stay committed, monitor your progress, and use what you learn as feedback to adjust your course.

And don't change that path unless you decide it is necessary.

I remember not long after I became a restaurant owner, I went to a meeting with an outside accountant I had hired to advise me. We were sitting in one of our McDonald's in Boston, the accountant loaded down with ledgers and notes. I asked her what she thought about a proposal I had shared with her the day before.

"Pete," she said, "I've looked at the numbers…." Her voice trailed off.

"And?" I said.

"I don't think you should proceed with this loan just now," she said. "I'm not sure that your cash flow at this particular time could allow you to meet the obligations you'll incur."

It's funny how nobody delivers bad news unvarnished. They never start with "don't do it." They always dress it up, talk fancy, trot out the big words, and try to sound like what they imagine an expert sounds like. I was never a fan.

"So don't do it?" I said.

"Yes," she said. "Don't do it."

I wanted her advice; I was grateful for it – I was paying for it! – and I knew she was giving me her best professional judgment.

I also knew that "best professional judgment" is a nice way of saying *don't take chances.*

She had professional skills in accounting that I did not have. Her counsel was not to be rejected out of hand and not to be taken lightly. So I looked at her numbers myself. There were a few things I disagreed with and others that were a matter of judgment or interpretation.

I realized that my accountant, whom I paid for her best judgment, was giving me only that, her judgment – her opinion.

This consultation had drifted from her professional expertise about her area of knowledge into her subjective opinion about mine.

The question at hand, the securing of a significant loan for expansion, wasn't a matter of the black-and-white, yes-or-no questions that are answered by the rules of accounting. This was a business decision, which is a matter of professional judgment, tolerance for risk, and the experience-based intuition that only the owner of a business can really feel and truly know.

I gave her the respectful consideration she deserved, taking a moment or two to review the paperwork and collect my thoughts. But it took only an instant to know what I was going to tell her.

"Thanks for taking a look," I said, "but here's what we're going to do. We're going to go to the bank, and I'll do the talking. I'm going to explain how our cash flow will be enough to meet the bank's requirements and that, given the state of the business, I'll be able to make these loan payments."

"But the accounting, here on the paper–"

"You're right about how things look on paper," I said, "but that's only on paper. There are lots of other considerations. There are even other ways to look at the problem. There are, in fact, other ways we could put the problem down in black and white."

"It's not just that I want to do this," I continued. "And it's not just that I believe we can do this. When I consider every factor – not just those I've shared with you as my accountant – when I consider all that, I *know* we can do this."

We went to the bank. Sure enough, they were persuaded by my case and made the loan to me. And I paid it back in a timely way, as I knew I could.

Progress requires taking risks, and wise risk-taking begins with appreciating the value of your knowledge and instincts. I could have just accepted the advice of an outside expert and pressed "pause" on my plans, but that wasn't the smart play. This happened to be a risk worth taking.

This is something I learned from my father. He was not a well-educated man, but he taught me some valuable things, especially about business. In this case, he was eerily prescient. *Listen to your attorney*, he said. *Listen to your accountant. Listen to your advisors.*

Hear what they have to say, and take away what you need to know. But in the end, make your own decisions.

Own your business, own your future, own your success, and in this way, you will own your life. I've lived by that for a long time. Hire good people and hear them out, but never forget that they work for you, not the other way around. Make your own decisions.

FIND THE UPSIDE IN EVERY PROBLEM

Any family doctor will tell you that a lot of what they do is the same thing over and over. Sure, they see exotic or unusual cases once in a while, but for every one of those comes a dozen far more common maladies such as a sore throat, a broken limb, or an infection. It's the same for plumbers and electricians. The occasional surprise is out there, but mostly there is a handful of similar issues that come up every day.

The same thing happens to managers, and on that hangs a way to improve your management skills.

Seeing the same thing and getting it right each time builds confidence, but it also gives you the chance to improve at the thing you do the most. For each occurrence of that thing, you're familiar with, you don't have to spend much time figuring out how to fix it. So take each recurrence as a moment to find how this one might be a little different, and how you might respond a little more effectively or just a bit faster.

Treat every problem as an opportunity to motivate and educate yourself.

Early in my career, I was overseeing several suburban McDonald's restaurants. I did well with that so Mr. McCoy gave me more responsibility and assigned me to restaurants in the city of Boston.

I'll be honest with you. In those days, the big city was foreign to me. I'd come from Sicily as a kid, but that was a long time before. By this time, my world was the suburbs. I was a little nervous to work in the city. I assumed that the rhythm would be different, the people would be different, and the demands would be different.

It was the same job as the one I had in the suburbs, but a little different, as I would soon find out.

Living in the heart of any big city brings out a kind of toughness that is unfamiliar to those of us who see the city as only an occasional destination. Things really do move faster, and the environment is less forgiving. Some people thrive in it, a few don't, but no one knows how they'll do until they're in it.

I remember one of my first crew meetings I had at a McDonald's on Tremont Street. I was talking to the crew and managers about the importance of quality and how much emphasis we put on food safety.

"These standards matter," I said. "We have to adhere to standards so every meal we sell to a customer is excellent. That means that if a sandwich or some other item is held for longer than the set period, we have to discard it. I'm not sure we're always doing that."

At that, a gentleman stood up, obviously offended and already angry. He looked me right in the eye and said, "Are you talking about me?"

I'll tell you: it took my breath away. I was not used to people questioning me, especially in a meeting, especially in a restaurant where I was in charge. I was unaccustomed to being challenged, and never had I experienced a physical threat to back it up.

I took a deep breath. Fortunately, the years already under my belt of managing people told me by instinct how to respond – this was a familiar problem, just a little different.

"My goal is to lead this team so that we deliver quality to our customers," I said. "We do that now, and what I want is even more consistent quality. So you're going to have to hear me out, and that goes for everyone. As for you, sir, if you want to talk about this more, we can do it after the meeting. I'm glad to do it, glad to explain anything you like, and I mean that."

"But for now I'm not going to hold us up. Let's proceed."

After the meeting was over, I didn't wait for this man to come to me. I didn't want him to walk away and stew. This needed to be dealt with – rather, I needed to deal with it myself. Right after we finished, I went up to this fellow so he could have the opportunity to say what was on his mind. He talked, I talked, and we both listened. I'm proud to say that this gentleman went on to become a wonderful employee who stayed with us for years – a truly valuable part of our team, and a contributor to excellence.

Dealing with employees who feel singled out or slighted was a familiar problem, but I took it as an opportunity to learn. It turns out that my concerns about going from the suburbs to the city were well placed, but I had it turned around. Instead of thinking just about my reaction to them, I should have thought about their reaction to me. It had little to do with the city-versus-suburb difference and everything to do with good, old-fashioned empathy. I needed to put myself in the place of someone else because they weren't used to a manager like me who says what is on his mind. What I meant as clear direction was taken as disrespect, which of course was the opposite of what I intended.

I learned a lot that day about managing people and communicating with them, not just speaking my mind.

In other words, I took a problem and made it into an opportunity.

AFTERWORD

DO UNTO OTHERS, THEN FORGET IT

I dedicated this book to my parents with the phrase in Italian, *Fare del bene agli altri, per poi dimenticarsene.*

It means "Do unto others, then forget it." The meaning is as simple as it sounds. You don't have to dig. It's just this: be kind and move on. Don't wait around for whatever nice thing you did to be repaid. Stop treating kindness as a transaction with someone else, and start treating it as a choice you make for yourself.

The more you give in this way – without the expectation of anything in return – the greater the satisfaction you will find, and the greater the peace of mind. You may soon come to think of being kind to others as something more for you than for others.

Imagine the mental energy you'll take back when you're moving on to the next thing instead of keeping score, waiting for your reward for each good deed.

Stop thinking of the kindness you give as an invoice for payment. Start thinking of it as a gift. Though there will be benefits.

Think about the people you know who are generous in this way. You admire them, don't you? You consider them to be role models. You assume they are more comfortable in their skins, happier with their lives, and less worried than you are about what other people think.

All that is exactly the case.

Where once you were frustrated by not getting "paid back," now you're not only avoiding disappointment: you're also avoiding the anger and resentment that came with it.

Where once you felt depressed from being unappreciated, you're now taking your pleasure from the act itself: you feel appreciated because you now better appreciate your own attitude.

Start with the simple things.

When someone speaks with you, give them your full attention. Put down the phone. Turn off the email. Look them in the eye. Listen.

When someone tells you their plans, encourage them. There will be plenty of others to tell them why it won't work, what they lack, or how long the odds are. Instead, be the rare person who tells them that it just might work and that they are just the person to do it.

Give people the benefit of the doubt, even when they've let you down in the past. We tend to live up to or down to the expectations of others. Show them trust. A lot of things that aren't true start to become true when we choose first to believe them.

Apologize when you're wrong. Accept your errors, and apologize. Be sincere, then forgive yourself, and – you know what to do:

forget it.

If there's a way to say yes, say yes. It might mean changing your plans, spending a little money, or doing things differently than usual, but your small sacrifice could be the key to someone else's great success.

I imagine you're getting the idea. Put others first. And when you do, appreciate the positivity you've created – then move on.

I'm not perfect at this, but I don't know anyone who is. Yet we try, and that's enough. Whatever good you and I put into the world by the end of the day is more than was there back at sunrise.

Take it from me, you want to look back and know in your bones it was a good life. But to have a good life, you have to live a good life. *Live a good life. Live your best life.*

When you do unto others, you're doing for yourself.

Magnifico!

THE END

Made in the USA
Middletown, DE
27 September 2023

39541303R00176